Joseph Hine Rylance

Christian Rationalism

Essays on Faith and Unbelief

Joseph Hine Rylance

Christian Rationalism
Essays on Faith and Unbelief

ISBN/EAN: 9783743367128

Manufactured in Europe, USA, Canada, Australia, Japa

Cover: Foto ©Lupo / pixelio.de

Manufactured and distributed by brebook publishing software (www.brebook.com)

Joseph Hine Rylance

Christian Rationalism

CHRISTIAN RATIONALISM

ESSAYS ON MATTERS IN DEBATE
BETWEEN
FAITH AND UNBELIEF.

BY J. H. RYLANCE, D. D.

PUBLISHED AT THE BIBLE HOUSE, NEW YORK, BY THOMAS WHITTAKER, 1898.

COPYRIGHT, 1898,
BY THOMAS WHITTAKER

"Reason is the only Faculty we have wherewith to judge of anything, even Revelation itself."—*Butler.*

CONTENTS

	PAGE
ESSAY I.	
ON FREE THOUGHT	7
ESSAY II.	
ON REASON AND FAITH	37
ESSAY III.	
ON INSPIRATION AND INFALLIBILITY	69
ESSAY IV.	
ON THE RACKING DOUBT	107
ESSAY V.	
ON EXISTING DISSENSIONS BETWEEN SCIENCE AND RELIGION	143
ESSAY VI.	
AN HISTORIC FOOTHOLD FOR FAITH	187

I.

ON FREE THOUGHT.

It might prove instructive, if one cared to go into the question, to ascertain how free thought ever came to be identified with infidel thought, or a freethinker with a disbeliever in the doctrines of Christianity. So it is, however, as we all well know, to the very serious prejudice of Christ's religion; the appropriation of the title of "Freethinkers" by the men who deny the Gospel of Jesus seeming to imply, that those who accept it do so on terms which will not bear the application of free thought; or, if Christian believers may be credited with thinking at all, then are they to be counted slavish thinkers; or held to be under bonds to some authority which discountenances thinking.

Some such assumption as that may be detected in the men who jingle the phrases Free Thought, Free Thinker, Free Religion, in our ears to-day; with hinted scorn of those who are thus supposed to have a dread of all mental freedom, as affecting the interests of Christianity. Talk and insinuation of such purport circulate very freely about us; specially in circles of sceptics of a certain intellectual grade; the insults so offered to men of positive Christian convictions being less noticeable than the childish egotism of the men who so talk. The phrase "Free Thought" has come to have a touch of cant about it, indeed, very distasteful to men of discreet minds, whether Christian or infidel. There is a tone in the common use of it, which arrogates for all freethinkers a superior order of intellectual power. Free thinking is to supply the solvent for every problem that perplexes us, and to set the whole world right on all questions that trouble it; the subjects of these anticipations forgetting the fact, that the ultimate value of thought of any sort, is to be estimated, not by the quality or the circumstance of its *freedom*, so much, but by its clearness, and its soundness, and its logical consistency. For freedom is simply the space, so to speak, in which thought operates. What thought can *do*, in the widest sphere of activity conceded to it, is the question. It may be narrow, with the largest possible room round it; or frivolous, conceited, blind. Or it may be ill-balanced, vapory, and run to riot. Freedom is only a condition, in other words, either of thought or of action. How will a man use his freedom, is the question. For the freedom itself supplies no sure guarantee that the thinking will be worth anything, how free soever it may be. There may be just as thorough a spirit of bigotry, indeed, in the man who boasts that he is a freethinker, as in the man who looks upon all free thought with a devout horror.

Yet must it not be inferred from this that it is ever just or expedient to repress by force the utterance of opinion or conviction in a community, as long as vital interests are not seriously threatened. We must accept freedom of thought with all the extravagances it may lead to, as long as it does not violently interfere with thinkings that the freethinker might not call free. Mr. Mill, in his admirable little book on "Liberty," made out a very good case in behalf of freedom of opinion, and of debate. The truth therein contended for did not need, however, the pains which the philosopher bestowed in its defence; the liberty he so cogently contended for having been very generally conceded by the governments of all free countries, even in his own time. All intelligent and open-minded men are substantially agreed to-day, that religious and social doctrines and institutions must be maintained by other means than a blind force, if they are to be maintained at all. Rulers both of Churches and of States ought to have learned that by this time. For whenever force has been applied to curtail the free action and circulation of opinion, the policy, in all free countries, at least, has not only failed, in the long run, but has secretly fostered the evil it was intended to destroy; by begetting resentments and a general sense of injustice in men's minds. While men remain in a state of intellectual childhood a policy of coercion may seem to succeed; the imposing of an implicit subjection being a comparatively easy task in the case of children, but it is ofttimes hard in the case of grown men. A paternal government has always seemed to be the best for all concerned, as long as subjects have been content with their swaddling clothes; but a time comes, in the development of nations as of individual men, when the garments of the child are found not to fit the stalwart limbs of the man. And then there is apt to be some rending done, if the swaddling clothes are not quietly laid aside in time. There was a very violent rending of such raiment in Europe toward the close of the last century; the immediate results being most marked in a nation in which there had been working for some time a strong and an acute intelligence. For long the rulers had gone on ruling " by the grace of God," as they said; and fearfully dark and cruel things had been done under the assumed sanction; till the people, or the more enlightened among them, became sceptical of the high claim, and a reaction set in. For a time it was repressed: then compromise was tried: but the weight of waters steadily gathered behind the embankments of authority, till they yielded; and the floods went thundering down pleasant valleys, and across fertile plains, till the very globe seemed to shake to its centre. One of the rulers had said—"After me the deluge"; and the deluge had come. Or, in a figure more familiar, possibly, to some of my readers, the civil and ecclesiastical engineers of those times, had for long sat smiling upon the safety-valve of the State machine; till the pent-up power beneath blew them and the machine into the air! Developed powers in peoples must have larger room provided for their safe working; one great need in those who guide the energies of a nation, political, social, or religious, being a quickness of discernment

"When to take
Occasion by the hand, and make
The bounds of freedom wider yet."

Those bounds do not admit of very much widening for the people of these United States in the *political* sphere; the largest possible liberty being guaranteed to all citizens by the fundamental provisions of the instrument which makes us a Commonwealth. But liberty of *thought* is still dreaded by multitudes among us, as somehow perilous to faith and piety; all kinds of pleas and prophecies being heard, specially from our schools of theology, to bring it into discredit. While in lands where the Church retains anything of her old tyrannous power, stronger measures are still sometimes directed against heretical opinion. The folly of such attempts should be obvious, however, if only from the fact that *thinking* is just that one prerogative of man which cannot be controlled by force. Statecraft, or priestcraft, may bind and bend the *body* into all sorts of subservient attitudes; by loading it with chains, or by putting it under the grim and grinding rack—for our frail humanity shrinks from pain—but we cannot touch the *mind* by such clumsy devices. You may make cowards, slaves, hypocrites, by penal coercion; but you cannot beget a single sentiment or conviction in the reason or in the conscience of men by either threat or penalty. It is not only cruel, therefore, but it is silly to resort to such methods of manipulating men's minds; while as to practical consequences I venture to affirm, that the evils traceable to free thinking are a thousandfold less hurtful to Religion, than the evils that have sprung from blindly attempting to repress free thinking.

Ecclesiastical rulers have assured us again and again, very solemnly, that if men should be suffered to do their own thinking without dictation or restraint, the world would soon be deluged with a licentious infidelity. But Ecclesiasticism likes to frighten people, for its own ends. Let the prediction be brought to the test of fact—for coercion has had ample scope to exhibit its virtues—and all the foolish fears which orthodoxy inspires into timid souls, touching this question as so many others, will vanish. What have been the fruits of coercion in Italy, in France, in Spain, or wherever the tyranny of power has tried to repress free inquiry? Is Christian faith firmer in those countries to-day than in parts of Christendom where the claims of private judgment have been respected? Is there more of religious reverence, of devoutness, or of obedience to Divine Commandments there than elsewhere? Is the Bible more revered from men having been forbidden to read it? Or is the Church stronger there in popular favor and affection, from men having been compelled to accept its mandates in dumb submission? Let the terribly irreligious condition of vast sections of continental Europe answer; with their populations utterly alienated from the Church; many being filled with a deep detestation of the very name of religion. Which desperate condition of things is largely traceable to the policy which has tried to stifle all inquiry, outside of the very narrow limits allowed by the Church; to a policy which has denied men light lest they should see, and denied them knowledge lest they should know; and which now has the audacity to impute the evils it originated, to the power that has at length risen up in protest against its tyranny and deceit!

Nor need we marvel if men, moved by a passionate hate of unreality and imposture, have rushed to the wildest extremes of opinion and feeling as to all things taught in the name of Religion. When those who have long lived in darkness are suddenly brought into light, the eye is bewildered, and the brain sometimes dizzy, for a while. Or when the limb that has long worn a shackle is released from the coil, the nerves are unsteady till strengthened by use. But there is surely occasion of good hope, for those who believe both in Christ's religion and in mental freedom, in the fact, that where the latter is to-day allowed the widest range, the former has its firmest foundation.

I have myself, therefore, no sympathy with those who would lay any unfair restraint upon the free play of thought in our time; or with those who apply opprobrious epithets to men calling themselves "freethinkers"; or with the priests or preachers who tell us of a fiery and everlasting vengeance, awaiting all who doubt the generally accepted creeds of their churches. If such weapons were ever of any really good service in the maintenance of Christian Faith, they are worse than useless to-day. The rapid spreading of intelligence; the progress of democratic doctrines and institutions in all enlightened States; the sense of self-ownership, so to speak, that has everywhere taken possession of men's minds, and of rights which they deem their due, and of responsibilities in others toward them;—these advances are rapidly rendering the task of authority to maintain its old imperious attitudes hopeless. Statesmen, of the old conservative order; priests, who look upon themselves as set to insist upon ancient decrees without abatement or qualification; "privileged classes," who have hitherto had such a pleasant time of it in the many being willing to serve them in almost dumb subjection;—all these begin to look round them in fear, upon the independent tone and bearing of the emancipated throng; wondering why men cannot be content with the old "divinely ordered" condition of things, and with the methods which once worked so smoothly, seemingly, in the management of the world's affairs. Even so. One is almost moved to pity, at sight of men so bewildered 'mid the altered relations and commotion of our age; yet are the ignorance and cowardice of such men really worthy of scorn. For such commotion was sure to ensue "in the process of the suns"; and the worst is not yet, probably. Were it not fitting to say, that men in positions of influence would more worthily occupy themselves in educating and guiding the energies newly let loose in society, than in foolishly trying to repress them? or in speaking evil of them? Yet is this the temper and disposition of many of our fellow citizens of character and culture; apprehending, as they do, serious evils to religion from the intellectual ferment of the time.

The battle is between Authority, with all its prestige and all its venerable sanctions, on the one hand, and what is called Individualism on the other; this "*bête noire*" of Individualism being an ignorant, lawless, and desperately revolutionary creature, as depicted by those who dread it. Yet is it simply the right which a man claims to do his own thinking, and to draw his own conclusions, and to follow thinkings and conclusions out in life, so long as he does not hurtfully intrude upon the thinkings and conclusions of his neighbor in so doing. But what exposures and denunciations of Individualism we hear from pulpits, and get through "the religious press"; an American prelate having lately leveled a book at the creature, in which he professes to "strike at its core." But who or what is it that condemns Individualism but Individualism?—as represented by some priest, or preacher, or professor of divinity. Or the condemnation comes from a *collection* of individualisms, as seen in some conference, or synod, or council. But though it may be sometimes true that "in a multitude of counsellors there is wisdom," yet a multitude of fallibilities can never yield us *in*fallibility.

But I may be reminded that priestly Individualism, representing the historic Christian Church, rests back upon a vast, consolidated, and trustworthy Authority; before which all right-minded men might reasonably be expected to stand reverently silent.

Well; I do not myself deny the existence of such an historical "deposit," upon which Faith may draw to some extent; but I do deny that inquiry can be logically so precluded. For what is Authority, even of the very highest order known to us, but the gathered up and formulated opinions, testimonies, judgments—all duly endorsed, let us say—of *individual men?*—of martyrs, saints, apostles, prophets? such opinions, testimonies, judgments, gathering not only bulk, but moral weight, as the fears and respect and reverence of men gathered round them, in the course of the centuries. Let us even say, that the first witnesses to truths now enjoined as authoritative, were unimpeachable witnesses; yet must a man somehow decide for himself to-day, that their testimony, *as delivered to us*, is genuine, and adequate for the purpose, or purposes, for which it is cited. And thus we get Individualism again; in the necessary work of authenticating the evidence on which Authority rests its claims; the only plea that can be preferred in favor of the maintenance of the old docile submissiveness amounting to this, that men and women are to yield to Authority in settlement of all disputes affecting Religion *because its utterances are authoritative!* an argument which were as good for the Koran as it is for the

Bible; or for Buddhism as it is for Christianity. But more, along this line of caveat. Granted that the authority alleged as good ground for faith to-day, was sufficient and irrefutable at the first; yet will it be conceded by all men of intelligence and candor, that in the vast, miscellaneous mass of doctrines and dogmas and conceits commonly enjoined by Authority in this age, there are many things of human invention, and some purely fictitious; while others have had an exaggerated importance attached to them; all such admixtures and perversions requiring discrimination in those who would have the truth free from error; which sifting process involves the exercise of the dreaded Free Thought, or the assertion of the detested Individualism.

But why should it be assumed that Individualism is necessarily the unruly and destructive power it is represented to be, by those who seemingly stand in terror of it? It may safely be contended, on the contrary, I think, that there are few men, except the light-minded and self-conceited,—and with such men we have nothing to do in this discussion,—who are not willing to show a proper deference to Authority, when of a kind to inspire an intelligent respect; aye, even to Authority in the shape of a tolerably well-founded *tradition*, in any sphere of thought or investigation where tradition can claim to be considered at all. Let it come to this, then, that men shall be suffered to think freely, and freely to assert the conclusions they may reach touching Religion; the necessary consequence would not be intellectual anarchy, much less the destruction of all faith in the foundation facts and doctrines of Christ's Gospel; but simply a larger variety of opinion, perhaps, about matters which could not command evidence sufficient to beget definiteness of conviction. As to all essential things enjoined or taught by Jesus and His Apostles, however, faith would be stronger and more influential, because intelligent and free. Take away all dictatorial authority affecting religious beliefs, and all the evidence upon which those beliefs profess to rest would remain to us; begetting conviction in all men capable of appreciating the evidence; and leading to a general convergence of opinions and feelings sufficient to satisfy all reasonable requirements as to a "Unity of the Faith." But why do I speak hypothetically? It *is* thus that all intelligent belief knits itself together and gathers into a body even now; Authority having very much less to do with the matter than those men think who dwell on its virtues so appealingly. It might allay the fears of such men, somewhat, would they only recollect, that there are *conservative* instincts in human nature, which will always secure a prevailing respect for truths, and for institutions, and for customs, that have the attributes of reasonableness and wholesomeness visibly in them; while there will always remain *moral* authority, springing out of the very nature of the truths which Christianity proclaims, fortified by their necessary influence in and over individual men and society at large, sufficient to make itself a governing power in the world.

What we really have occasion to fear in the present unsettled condition of the public mind touching matters of a religious nature, is such a preaching and teaching of Authority as may spread the suspicion abroad that the faith of the Christian world rests on nothing deeper than Authority; or, that at the touch of Free Thought all the creeds of Christendom would melt into mist. Conceits of such sort are already harbored, indeed, by multitudes of our fellows; owing, very largely, to the foolish fears exhibited by our orthodox Scribes as to the ravages threatened by Free Thinking—these teachers thereby abjuring all title to be considered freethinkers themselves. Whereas their own faith, and their very trust in Authority, would be found, upon the issue of a thorough analysis of such faith and trust, to have no better guarantees of validity than those that can be made good by free thinking; and which the most fervent believer in Authority must be supposed to have actually so made good, to escape the scorn of discerning men.

There is really nothing left for us, then, constituted and conditioned as we are,—let men lament it as they may—but to seek, mid all the embarrassments of this probationary state, to know the mind and will of the Great God toward us; whether written in books, or on rocks, or in the constitution and intuitions of the human soul; and the sooner our religious guides begin to suffer such seeking to go on without hindrance, and without objection, the better will it be for the cause which they represent. No man can dictate to me what I shall hold as essential to acceptance with God, till he has submitted his credentials in proof of his right to dictate; investigation into the reliability and sufficiency of which supposes, of course, the concession of all the rights claimed by Freethinkers.

But a difficulty emerges here; or rather, a difficulty must now have attention that has been pressing for notice for some distance back in this discussion, as the reader has no doubt felt; which difficulty may be best indicated, perhaps, by a question as from the lips of a free-thinking friend. "How are you going to reconcile the claims of free thought, which you seem to concede," such an one might say to me, "with the predetermination of the conclusions which the Freethinker must reach to be acceptable to God, as you Christians talk? It seems to me, and to those who hold with me," our free-thinking friend might go on to say, "that you liberal Christians are 'playing fast and loose' with us. On the one hand, you allow that a man has the right to the free use of his intellectual faculties in religious questions; but on the other, you lay down beforehand the results which the inquirer must reach, to escape the 'eternal death' you have in store for him, should he reach other conclusions than those you prescribe, or that your religion prescribes. But that, it seems to us, is a concession with a very illogical stipulation attached to it." Now, the exception is fairly taken and stated, it must be allowed; and is deserving of as fair and frank an answer. It is an exception that has been an occasion of much mental perplexity, I suspect, in men who, while retaining devout respect for prescribed truth, acknowledge the rights of free Inquiry. How can these seemingly conflicting attitudes of mind be reconciled?

Well; it must be assumed, in the first place, and the assumption must be steadily borne in mind, that the Free Thought which we are to suppose to be bent upon finding out the truth or the untruth of the essential things in Christianity, is of a *sober, intelligent, and*—may I not stipulate?—*reverent* caste and character. That preliminary being conceded, as being required by the nature of the problem to be solved, it will be further allowed, I am sure, that the quest after the truth belief of which Christianity insists upon shall be *thorough*, before a man can be suffered to settle down in unbelief unblamed. Then,—and to this condition the most resolute Freethinker will bring no objection, I take it—that the process of truth-seeking shall be conducted with a *vigilant fidelity;* with the mind of the inquirer open to every ray of light, come whencesoever it may; and with the heart free from all perverting impurities, and possessed of the requisite moral susceptibilities for truth of the kind now in question to make its proper impression upon the nature. For the *heart*, as most men of a ripened discernment have learned, has a great deal to do in rendering *moral* investigations successful. Then one other condition will be granted me, I have no doubt, viz: that the *life of the inquirer shall be one of practical submission to the great laws of Christian duty*, while the inquiry is going on; according to an authority which the Freethinker may not count divine, but which, in this case, asserts a principle of profound importance in ethical science: the principle expressed in the words —"*If any man will do His will, (God's* will), *he shall know of the doctrine that it is of God.*"

Now, holding that I have made no unfair demand in this preliminary statement of terms, I may here ask—where is the man who has conscientiously and thoroughly complied with these terms, and yet remains in a state of settled unbelief? I do not know the man; though I have had a good deal to do with unbelievers, of every grade, and of every shade of opinion. Somewhere there has been inattention, neglect, or possibly graver shortcomings, on the part of the man who has missed his way in the process of truth-seeking; or he had surely come upon evidence enough to give him pause, at least, in his denial of the testimony of Jesus. It will be answered, I know, that this, in effect, is the old imputation upon the honesty of the unbeliever. I am too discriminating, while I know too much of the pain and trouble that some men have endured in quest of rest for their doubts, to put the conclusion in that bald way. But I am compelled, as a Christian, and as a man, to attribute the failure to find ground for faith in the New Testament revelation of Love and Righteousness, not to the fact that such ground is wholly wanting, but to the inquirer's having failed, somewhere, to comply with conditions upon which faith is suspended, in the economy witnessed to in the Gospel of Jesus Christ. Most assuredly may it be said, that of those who deny the essential facts and doctrines of Christianity, few can be found whose denial is traceable to searching thought of any sort. The many err through moral indolence, or from lack of intellectual seriousness; through hasty assumptions, or a captious conceit; or from foolishly imputing the foibles and faults of so-called Christians to the religion which condemns those faults! To build conclusions affecting such weighty interests upon such flimsy foundations, however, is surely unworthy of a man who calls himself a *free* thinker. Thought with such an one, I should rather say, is narrow, crooked, self-willed, and therefore blind. And upon such a state of mind, God Almighty were impotent to produce the conviction of faith.

But much of this is beside the mark, as a

contribution toward the confutation of the contentions of Infidelity. What is needed is, that the two parties to the debate, the Freethinker and the Christian Apologist, should somehow get at a better understanding of each other's position, and of each other's claims; or of the real question, or questions, they are supposed to be discussing.

Specially should the Freethinker be given to know, through fair and explicit presentations of the truth, that it is not faith in all the theories, speculations, far-fetched deductions, of our schools of theology, or in matters in any way necessarily doubtful, that Christianity insists upon; but upon faith in the vital and vitalizing facts and doctrines of Christ's Gospel, *which are few;* which distinction glances at an occasion of a vast amount of unbelief just now prevalent. For there are many things in our theologies and in our ecclesiasticisms which bewilder and vex men of an independent temper; they in their heat and haste dismissing *all* religious claims as unworthy of serious regard; the representatives of Religion having given the world to understand, that all the legendary incredibilities of early Jewish writings, with their sanctions of atrocities at which we shudder, and with all the groundless decrees of Church councils since Christ came;—all these are to be received without question, and approved without scruple, say our priests and preachers, before men or women may presume to call themselves Christians!

No marvel that Infidelity is rife. It is the old story, which the records of human experience tell so distressingly; but the Scribes, as of old, refuse to learn. The Church has *made* infidels by the hundred, and then has consigned them to the unquenchable fires for *being* infidels! The superstitions and impostures of the Romish Church of the time, and of anterior times, were chiefly responsible for the infidelity of M. De Voltaire. It was these which armed the keen-witted man with those shafts of criticism and of scorn, which he fired with such telling effect into the system which priestcraft had built up and administered in that age. While Protestant preachers have been doing the same thing, in their own way, for generations, as they are doing to-day. They tell the Freethinker, that every syllable in the Bible is "inspired," and *equally* inspired; and therefore of divine, and unvarying, and everlasting authority. Which is taken to mean, which is commonly *intended* to mean, that every utterance which we find recorded within the bindings of the Sacred Book, and every transaction going to make up its history, and every precept and sentiment of the many and very variegated speakers and writers represented in the Volume,—that all these are divinely true, and of unchanging obligation.

Nor is there to be any discrimination in the valuing of the statements or precepts: no asking from whom they came, or when they were spoken, or for what particular purpose: no seeking to learn, for instance, whether any of them have become obsolete for Christians, in whole, or in part. Neither is there to be any discrimination in judging of their applicability to life as we know it to-day. No: we have simply to open the Bible, and to take whatever we find there, and esteem it divine. And the Freethinker takes the preacher at his word; and goes and makes his selections—*for uses of a kind which the preacher did not contemplate.* He gathers out of the Volume the story of the *apple and the serpent;* with that of *the woman turned into a pillar of salt;* with the account of *the wholesale slaughter of the Canaanites,* and of *the treacherous murder of Sisera;* never forgetting the legend of *Jonah and the whale;* citing with relish the maledictions of angry Psalmists, and their invocations of unutterable calamities upon their enemies; all which "elegant extracts," with a hundred others of like tone and character, the Freethinker takes and flings abroad upon uproarious audiences in our Theatres and Lecture Halls; holding out the Bible at arm's length, and crying—" *There's* your Book of God!"

It is all very sad; but the most afflicting thing in or about the whole business is, that Christian Teachers have, in effect, put these ugly weapons into the hands of their adversaries; by telling them, or by suffering them to assume, that Christianity requires its disciples to believe, and to approve, all the incredible and atrocious things of which we read in certain fragments of early Human History; and this spite of the vehement protest of Jesus, repeated again and again,—"Ye have heard that it was said by the ancients, ($\tau o \hat{\iota} s$ $\dot{a} \rho \chi a \acute{\iota} o \iota s$) . . . thou shalt hate thine enemy. But *I* say unto you, Love your enemies!" Is it not about time that these mischievous stupidities on the part of our religious Teachers had an end?

But if something is due to the Freethinker toward the attainment of a better understanding between himself and the worthier order of Christian Apologists in these debates, very much is also due from him to his adversaries. He should somehow become aware of the very considerable fact, and should somehow come to an easy practical acknowledgment of it, that the high and serious concerns he contends about are not to be settled by an embittered impetuous judgment; nor are they to be estimated, he ought to learn, according to what weak, or fanatical, or blindly dogmatic men may say about them.

Freethinkers must become discriminating in their judgments of the men they oppose, and of the doctrines they would destroy, and of the principles they would uproot: must cease from the vulgar blatant abuse now so common among them: must exchange declamation for argument, and an iconoclastic fury for something of the critical spirit; showing so much of moral sensibility toward interests at stake in the controversy between Faith and Unbelief, as may save them from the contempt due to all intellectual recklessness, and to all light-mindedness, in such grave debates. The religious world will continue to supply food for scoffing; but the scoffer is a type of man of which an age boasting its advancement can have but little need, or can consistently show much respect for. It is not enough for a man to come to us with large and noisy professions of Free Thought, when one sees at a glance that the man's thoughts are not worth a *sou* whether they be "bond or free." Much less may a man be suffered to go about, without rebuke, dealing out slanderous imputations against men of an unimpeachable uprightness, simply because they refuse to give up their faith in God. Yet has this temper been long dominant in all ranks of the Free-thinking world; even a man of the calibre of the late Mr. Froude having so far forgotten himself as to say, in a "fling" which he launched at the religious teachers of his time, that he would "like to know what those of the clergy thought"—on questions at issue between Faith and Infidelity,—"*whose love of truth was unconnected with their prospects in life:*" an insinuation which was simply base; and this from the Apologist of Henry VIII.! For my own part, I am free to say, from no morbid fear or passionate dislike of Free Thought, that I would rather betake myself to the little dark box of a Romish confessor to learn what Truth touching Religion is, than to the general run of our Freethinkers as they gather in noisy circles, or as they deal out their violent utterances through the Press.[1] While I

---

[1] See for representative specimens, M. Monteil's "*Catéchisme du Libre Penseur,*" *passim:* a book based upon the bold declaration of M. Gustave Flourens:—"Our enemy is God. Hatred of God is the beginning of wisdom. If a man would make true progress, it must be upon the basis of Atheism."

The Free Thought of England and America, is of a somewhat more reserved order.

would rather accept the Vatican "Syllabus" as the utterance of the highest attainable wisdom, than the rash and irrational criticism which arrogates the title of "advanced thought" to-day.

But we are not shut up to either of these alternatives, surely. Let not Christian men, from any insensate dread of Free Thinking, or by any indiscretion of act or of utterance, favor the assumption that we are. *Free* thinking is not necessarily *lawless* thinking. There is even a place for Authority in the education and direction of opinion and conduct; though it will never again sway men's minds as once it did. Luther little dreamed what an unruly spirit he was unchaining, when he began to assert the rights of "private judgment." The ecclesiastical thongs by which he and his co-workers sought to restrain private judgment within the bounds of a reasonable liberty, proved as ineffectual as the withes round the limbs of Samson did. The authority of the Bible turned out to be worth no more, in arrest of free inquiry, than the authority of the Church, for which it had been substituted, had proved. All which applies more forcibly to men to-day, and to social conditions now existing, than they did to the men and the conditions of the age of Luther. What then?

Are we out at sea without rudder to our craft, and without chart to guide us on our "dim and perilous way"? No: our plight is not as bad as that. Both Bible and Church may still render us good service in our quest after peace-giving Truth, and in the regulation of life's activities, if, while neither despising them, nor blindly revering them, we treat them with an intelligent respect; according to the light they shed on our pathway through the world, and according to the inspiration they may supply to our better moods of mind; we showing grateful regard, also, to all other lights that glimmer in the moral welkin; never forgetting the something within us that makes for righteousness. By a tolerably faithful following of these,—Bible, Church, Reason, Intuition, Moral Instinct, with the sweet solicitations of Nature,—we shall find the path open before us that leads through the strait gate into the city of God.

"Utterly impracticable and very dangerous latitudinarianism," some of my readers may exclaim; following the exclamation with an expostulation: "Of what use is such loose counsel for the ignorant masses of people about us to-day?" Well; as for them I have not very much fear; but I have a real concern for men and women who have enough of education to enable them to *see* difficulties in or about Religion, but not enough to enable them to see *through* them. But say that the many will always need the nursery treatment of Authority; yet is it daily becoming more and more evident, that for increasing numbers of men and women another sort of treatment is required in our time; to whom Christianity must be presented as a reasonable service before they will surrender themselves to its control. Let us, at least, have done with pathetic regrets that the good old days of an easy credulity are no more; and let us adjust ourselves and our apologetics to the facts of this closing Nineteenth Century. "Above all" —in the robust language of an English Freethinker,[1]—"let us dream no dreams, and tell no lies; but go our way, wherever it may lead, with our eyes open, and our heads erect; with no sophistry in our mouths, and no masks on our faces"; assured that the Great God will suffer no soul to fail of life hereafter, that has thus sought to know and to do His will.

[1] James Fitzjames Stephen, Q. C., in "*Liberty, Equality, and Fraternity,*" p. 334, Amer. Ed.

II.

ON REASON AND FAITH.

II.

ON REASON AND FAITH.

Or, on Reason *versus* Faith, I should rather say, with a heavy emphasis on the *versus*, were I, one of those who hold that the two are necessarily and essentially at enmity with each other. But as I am not, and as one chief purpose in my inditing this Essay is to show their friendliness and mutual helpfulness, I retain the simple conjunction.

Religiously orthodox writers show a marked partiality for Faith, very generally; asserting, or assuming, that it is, at least, superior to Reason, if not having sole right to be heard in the discussion of religious questions. An old English writer[1] asserts this claim to superiority somewhat strikingly. "Reason and Faith," says he, "resemble the two sons of the patriarch. Reason is the firstborn, but Faith inherits the blessing." Quaintly put, after the manner of the time, but betraying a purely

---

[1] Nathaniel Culverwell, *cir.* 1650, in his "*Light of Nature.*"
See a paper by Professor Henry Rogers, in the "*Edinburgh Review*" for Oct. 1849.

artificial conception of the relations which Reason and Faith sustain to each other in the moral economy of life; Faith having no such preëminence over Reason as that which the writer alleges; while no such arbitrary partiality is shown toward it by the Divine Ruler as seems to be implied in the pithy comparison of the old Puritan. Neither Reason nor Faith inherits any blessedness which properly belongs to the other. When a man has come to perceive that clearly; Reason and Faith being looked upon as organic powers in the constitution of human nature; each sustaining its own office, and doing its own work, in the moral education and direction of men; he is so far prepared to judge whatever claims may be preferred in behalf of Reason or of Faith intelligently, and impartially.

But few of those who take an active interest in these questions possess this qualification. They are partisans of this cause, or of that: champions of Reason, or defenders of Faith; the just claims of each often suffering in the strife. On the one hand we have the Christian apologist, of the orthodox type; who, in asserting the claims of Faith, commonly starts with assumptions which require to be established by Reason, before they can be admitted as grounds for inferences of the weight and width that apologists very generally proceed to draw from them. Claiming to be privileged with special light, however, or relying on an authority to which Reason is bound to submit, as he holds, the Biblical theologian refuses to have his postulates controverted. The more fanatical of these defenders of the Faith go to great lengths in such direction, at times; being guilty of gross offences against sound sense; speaking profanely of some of God's best gifts to men. "Human nature is carnal; man's judgment is perverted; his affections are depraved; no trust is to be reposed in any of the faculties or intuitions of his nature"—that is the style of talk to which we are commonly treated by "evangelical" theologians. The best endeavors of men to know the truth, or to do the right, are therefore to be looked upon with suspicion; a more reliable guide than Reason being lifted to supremacy by these zealots, in all religious investigations and debates. This guide is Faith, they tell us; Faith being, for many of them, a vague subjective emotion merely; while for others, it is reliance upon some external authority. For multitudes among us that authority is the Bible; for others, it is the Church. Or the authority inheres more immediately in a *person:* in a Pope, as the appointed organ of infallibility, in matters of a moral and religious order; or in "my priest," who, as a sort of little conduit, distributes to me such measure of the living water as he deems good for me; or in "my preacher," who generally condenses all the infallibilities of Books, and of Churches, and of Priests, into himself! In this way, from the theological side of the controversy, Faith is made to seem at enmity with Reason, wherever religious truth is concerned. In the affairs of common life, Reason may be followed, and trusted, by the devout and undevout alike. But she is not to gather up an inference, or to trace an analogy, which might tempt her upon forbidden ground— upon ground that is considered as belonging exclusively to Faith, that is. From this sphere, Reason would be repelled as an intruder; or, at most, called in to ratify conclusions dictated by Faith.

Such teaching is common, and very popular, as we know, in the believing world; such notions are in controlling ascendency in all our orthodox schools and churches; the pitiful results being obvious in the character, or lack of character, of so many who "profess and call themselves Christians"; especially among the weaker disciples of such schools. Whenever a reason is asked of these brethren for "the hope that is in them," instead of giving the best they can "with meekness and fear," the request is very generally resented, as an intrusion upon the forbidden ground I have just defined. "What!" replies the startled disciple, "do you not know that your question touches matters of Faith? What have you to do then with *reasoning* about such things?" And that sort of answer is deemed pertinent, and sufficient, quite commonly; not by the ignorant or superstitious only, but by men of penetration and good judgment both within and without the Churches. "On such things I never allow myself to reason," said a legal luminary of New York some time since; parrying a difficulty touching Faith which an eminent Scientist, then on a visit to this country, had started in talk.[1]

Now, there are, or there might be, circumstances 'mid which such an evasion might be allowable; for a man may have answers satisfactory to himself, as to matters of a difficult nature affecting his religious beliefs and feelings, but which he may be unable, or unwilling, to defend in formal argument. He may have reasoned the subject thoroughly out; but it does not follow

---

[1] The Scientist was Mr. Tyndall: the legal light, the then leader of the New York bar.

that he must go over all the evidence afresh, whensoever, or by whomsoever, it may be demanded of him. Or a man may have taken refuge from harassing doubts in the general concensus of the Christian world; or he may have found rest for mind and heart through the sweet and wholesome influences which Christ's truth has exerted upon his nature and conduct; and these, surely, together, or singly, may be allowed to suffice for a man; withóut his joining a perpetual debating society, where every little caviller has a right to catechize him about his faith. But if the gentleman who waived the scientist aside with the pious reply just given meant to say, that all reasoning upon things taught in the name of Faith is to be resented as intrusive; or that there are some matters so sacred in themselves, or from their associations, that all inquiry into them, or about them, is to be regarded as sinfully presumptuous; or if he meant to assert his belief in some authority above Reason, an authority having the right to settle all such matters dogmatically, in which settlement men are to acquiesce without question or misgiving; why, then, the answer to the scientist was not only evasive, but silly, spite of its piety. For there is no such authority lodged anywhere, to which men may resort for infallible answers to difficult questions, in theology or in any other sphere of thought, for the verifying of claims put forth as true in this world of conflicting opinions and professions—thus saving men the pain of seeking truth for themselves, should they be determined to enter upon, and to follow the perilous quest whithersoever it may lead. Men have felt such pain very acutely, at times; and have turned imploringly to this oracle or to that, where doubt might be dissipated, as they hoped, and the intellect be satisfied, and the conscience assured. But peace for the intellectually distressed is not to be so found, except of a stupid kind.

"But is not the Bible given to do these very things for us?" some one of my readers may be inwardly asking. To whom it might be answered, that the Bible may render such service to those who accept it passively, or unquestioningly; but what of the men who *will* start farther back than the mere declarations of the Book, and of the reputation in which it is held; asking—What *is* the Bible? and,— Whence did it get its authority to dictate conclusions to men, upon questions and interests so vast and so bewildering? Such men are not to be answered by simply saying—"The Bible is the Word of God"; for that is the very claim to be decided; which decision can only be reached, to the satisfaction of the sceptically inclined, through a process of investigation into the evidence alleged or allegeable in support of the Divine authority of the Book. That is conceded by the most cautious of our safe-going theologians; who tell us, so naïvely, that the office of Reason is to certify the claims of Divine Revelation, and to interpret the message which it brings to men. That bit of comfort used to be graciously conceded by theological experts to believers in Reason, as if that were a trifling matter to grant. Not only do such certifying and interpreting constitute a life-work full of difficulty to the best equipped, however, but the point to be noted here is this: that such concession to Reason really makes Reason the arbiter in all religious questions.

So too of the Church, to which others betake themselves for light, and peace, and a good hope. There are millions of men and women who accept its counsels, and creeds, and decrees, as final and absolute; all reasoning as to the reliability of such expedients being deemed impertinent by them. But the Church, it should be borne in mind, is an historic institution; whose credentials to teach must be authenticated by evidence which Reason must weigh and approve, before men can be summoned to sit at her feet in unquestioning silence.

All this will be counted strange, no doubt, as coming from one who seems to have some respect for Faith lying in the background of his thoughts; yet were it an inexplicable thing to me, that any thinking man should esteem what I am here saying strange, as applying to the Bible, or as applying to the Church. For with what are our Christian libraries filled? With catalogues, simply, of dogmas and doctrines and decrees, into the validity of which we are forbidden to inquire? Nay: but with stores of evidence and of argument and of criticism, very largely, which a learned and laborious Reason has gathered in confirmation and in elucidation of Christian *credenda*. And to these, as I understand her, the Church refers the inquirer for proof of her mission and authority, and for evidence authenticating the Bible as a revelation from God. Aye: even the Latin Church, most pronounced in her condemnation of Reason, filling her disciples with a flurry of fear on the mere mention of the word,—even she is driven, in the last resort, to fall back upon the very attestations which at other times she contemns. As witness the work of her scholars, and critics, and apologists—of which classes of craftsmen the Church of Rome has many—who, in their way, have been as busy and laborious as any, in vindicating by vast learning, and by far-reaching research, those foundations of Faith which lie beneath all assumed infallibilities, and of all dogmatic decrees; no less an authority than the late Cardinal Newman having told us, that even "the acts and words" of the sacred Pontiff "must be carefully scrutinized and weighed, before we can accept them as infallible." But scrutinizing and weighing are acts of the Reason, I take it. Upon Reason, therefore, the author of the "Grammar of Assent" being witness, ecclesiastical dogma inevitably depends.

What I am here contending for, then, not as a concession from authority of any sort, but as an organic necessity of the human mind, is asserted, or assented to, by those most jealous of Reason in matters of Religion. All men, of any tolerable degree of sagacity, holding whatever creed they may happen to hold, are compelled to admit in the long run, that the claims of Reason are first, and fundamental. "You must philosophize," said Aristotle; "and if any man say you must not philosophize, yet in saying that he doth philosophize": which, put into the speech of to-day, amounts to this:—You reason when you deny reason, or even when you deem reasoning sinful. For you must be moved by some reason, or reasons, surely, when you deny a man's right to reason upon religious dogmas. Men of intellectual acuteness, while holding strongly to Christian Faith themselves, have seen and allowed this. "Reason is the only faculty we have wherewith to judge of anything, even Revelation itself," said the author of the "*Analogy*"; while Locke has a touch of humor in his statement of the truth I am contending for. "Those who are for laying aside the use of Reason in matters pertaining to Revelation," said the author of the "Essay on the Human Understanding," "resemble one who should put out his eyes to make use of a telescope!"

But this statement of the case in behalf of Reason, may be construed as precluding all possible use for Faith, in the moral and spiritual education of men. I have seemed all along, perhaps, to be driving full upon that conclusion. Nay: I may even be taken to have asserted it, in saying that Reason is the arbiter of the truths upon which Faith rests. But the statement is not complete: Another side of the story has yet to be presented. Let those of my readers who may have been haunted with the suspicion, that all was being conceded by me that the baldest rationalism could demand, take breath here, therefore; for in what is yet to be said, material will be found for hope, I trust, that the cause of Faith admits of fair defence. Most of what I have said has been mainly preliminary to that end, indeed.

I have been trying to vindicate the rights of Reason, against those who, in the interests of Religion, as they think, are in the habit of doing those rights defiance; creating an impression upon the minds of their disciples that there is some sort of necessary antagonism between Reason and Faith; asserting the inference, very obvious to them, that the latter can only survive in its purity and power, when the former is denied all liberty to utter itself freely;—a fanatical conceit that is proving very hurtful to our Christian creed. I know something of the temptations that abound, for men of a devout temperament and disposition to take refuge from intellectual distractions affecting Religion in dogmatic authorities; some good people being in a state of lively alarm just now, from one of those crusades against all faith and piety which come and go in the lapsing of the centuries. The predominant tendencies of thought and research for some time, have been setting in a direction foreign, at least, to that which they had followed for ages. Science has been busy chiefly with material organisms, and with laws and forces assumed, by some, to be inherently of them; Philosophy, as distinct from Science, having lost much of the interest with which it once, and for long, inspired men. From the marvelous discoveries made in the prosecution of such aims, Science has become somewhat vain; speaking no longer in her old modest, cautious way, but in a dogmatic, intolerant, oracular way; showing herself particularly haughty toward Religion. Not on the ground that all matters in dispute between them have been heard and decided against Religion; but mainly from prejudices and presumptions—if one may be allowed to say so daring a thing. The spirit of the inductive philosophy seems to have almost forsaken us. What Butler complained of in the temper of the unbelief of his time, and which he did so much to correct, has reappeared in our own, but from somewhat different occasions. . . . "It has come to pass, I know not how," said that great thinker and dialectician, "that Christianity is not so much a subject for inquiry, but that it is now, at length, discovered to be fictitious"—that being just the temper that is felt to be so offensive, by many among us, in those who assail Christianity from a scientific standpoint to-day. Scarcely is there a truth that the Christian world has held sacred that is not rudely denied; scarcely a feeling it has cherished as holy which is not insulted. God, as a person, has been relegated out of the order and government of the Universe; matter being boldly credited with "the promise and potency of every form and quality of life!" Even so! No marvel if men of spiritual sensibility and experience have been startled and offended by such extravagances. But still more offensive to Christian men of taste and discernment, is the pity that is affected in infidel circles toward believers in Religion; with the covert sneer that one detects from time to time in the freethinker; with the bigotted babblement that prevails in little coteries of scientific neophytes! It is these things that do so much to drive men of Faith into extreme attitudes of mind toward a good deal of Modern Thought; and which tempt some of them to seek a refuge from all disturbances of their faith within enclosures from which all doubt and debate are shut out. Hence many of our so-called "conversions to Rome"; with renewed reverence for "pilgrimages" and "relics" in some of the oldest seats of Christian civilization; to the shame of all the centuries of boasted progress.

But these are unworthy ways by which to escape the dangers that threaten Christ's religion in our time. Faith must be vindicated by men of better intellectual build, of loftier courage, and of more reliable resources, than the men who shelter themselves beneath the skirts of priests. For it *can* be vindicated on the field of evidence and argument. But Faith as rationally defined, and as capable of being admitted among the ruling powers of a healthy moral life: Faith of the sort that Tillotson conceived of when he called it "a real persuasion about anything, whether grounded upon sense, or reason, or Divine Revelation." Our popular theologies are responsible for a vast amount of sheer fanaticism touching this matter of Faith; which would seem, as set forth by some of them, to be a blindly despotic power in the soul, unenlightened by reason, and unrestrained by law. But the Divine Ruler can no more be the Author of confusion in the Spiritual realm than in the realm of Nature. Faith is one member only in the organization of faculties and affections which constitute a complete humanity; filling its own place, and doing its own work in harmony with all the rest. Man cannot live by sense alone, or by the intellect alone, or by faith alone. The constitution of his nature, and the necessities of his manifold life, demand the concurrent and sympathetic exercise of all. And for this, it might seem the Almighty has hedged us about with difficulties, as incentives to an inquisitive Reason on the one hand, and as tests of a reverent Faith on the other—if one may venture a teleological guess; the ultimate purpose of the disciplinary process being what Butler calls—" an enlightened obedience to the will of God." The task of determining the just limits of each is difficult, but by this we are taught the need that exists in all moral investigations for attention and conscientiousness; lest Reason should be inflated by pride, and lest Faith should degenerate to credulity. Christian character approaches its highest perfection when both Reason and Faith contribute, each its proper quota of help, to its education and development. We need not become blasphemers in the name of Reason, nor cowards in the name of Faith.

But men are seldom tempted to yield to this weakness, except when Faith holds upon the higher truths of Religion. All other Faith is deemed a perfectly legitimate and a very rational feeling. Yet is Christian Faith, as an active principle or affection, essentially the same Faith as that which men are exercising and relying on in their daily doings, with no suspicion that it is a thing needing to be apologized for. It is simply the belief of what those who are possessed by it hold to be facts. Or it is trust in what they take to be reliable testimony: in testimony having the same guarantees for its trustworthiness as those which men are accustomed to rely on in accepting promises and pledges in the conduct of this world's affairs—promises and pledges of tremendous consequence sometimes. Faith of this sort is not only found to be a practicable principle or power in life, but an inevitably necessary principle; without which all confidence, and all coöperative activity, would be at an end; human society falling speedily into disorder and ruin. The man who should resolve to submit his thought and action only to the requirement of sense, or to the tests of science, or to the exactions of logical demonstration, would put himself out of gear with every form and function of life around him. All deep confidences, all high enterprises, all courage, and ambition, and hope, would die without Faith. For knowledge is personal, and therefore of limited range; so that if we are to see the world beyond our own narrow bounds, and to put ourselves into practical communications with it, we must see it with others' eyes, and feel it through the sensibilities of others; implicitly accepting testimony to multitudes of facts which would have no existence for us without Faith. Nay: the very sternest Positivist, who professes to abjure all such dependence, is busy in collecting and classifying his phenomena in serene reliance upon Faith: upon faith in the postulates and laws of "the higher reason"—those universal and necessary beliefs which have their evidence in themselves; such spontaneous intuitive trust being an organic necessity of our nature: preceding sense, and verifying its reports, and sanctioning its conclusions; testing even the discoveries of the scientist, and guiding the processes of the logician, and underlying the very axioms of the mathematician!

By constitution, then, and from necessities imposed upon us by our relationships and surroundings in life, we are creatures of Faith as well as of Reason. We must, or may, reason, then; and we must, or may, believe. Within certain limits only? "Yes," says the Theologian, "only within certain limits. You must not push your scrutinies into the sphere of things 'sacred': you must confine your reasonings within lines prescribed by the Church." While the Sceptic is equally dogmatic, in telling me that I must not believe in the "supernatural," that I must only believe what is reasonable; the two,—the Theologian and the Sceptic,—being, for once, thus far agreed. Now, the impracticability of the Theologian's counsel I have already made plain, I may assume. But that of the Sceptic is even more impracticable. I am not to believe in the Supernatural. I find a difficulty, however, in the way of my adopting this dictum; for I cannot draw a continuous line of distinction between the so-called supernatural and the natural; any more than I can draw such a line between things "sacred" and things "secular." Nor have I come upon any other man, or any body of men, very much more knowing than myself as to these matters. How am I to be made aware, then, when I come upon the forbidden territory in the advance of my beliefs? For advance they will, as my knowledge increases; showing me how many things are believable which in my ignorance I esteemed incredible, or which I deemed supernatural, it may be. As a matter of fact, the frontier of the supernatural has been pushed farther and farther back, as the domain of the natural has widened to men's apprehensions, all through what we call the ages of progress. Where the line of demarcation runs to-day, who shall pretend to say? As to whether there *is* any such line marking off the two domains, indeed, men of sense and penetration are becoming more and more sceptical; the more outspoken among them declaring, that this word "supernatural" is a mere conventionalism in speech—one of the many words by which we hide our ignorance while seeming all-knowing. There are no such frontiers as our professional talkers and writers have given unsophisticated hearers and readers to understand there are. The inconceivably vast, manifold COSMOS, the ORDERLY WHOLE, is *one domain;* we in our studies and manipulations of it breaking it up into departments for more convenient handling—that is all. Nor is the alternative limitation of my sceptical admonitor of much more avail. I am not to believe in the unreasonable. But who is to decide for me in all cases what is reasonable, or what is unreasonable? Myself? or some council of logical experts? Left to myself, I shall go on, of course, with the lights that may be in me, doing what I have all along been doing, what all men of an active, inquisitive intelligence are habitually doing:—balancing claims upon their beliefs; accepting some, denying others, according to preponderating probabilities weighing for or against the claims preferred; the dictum of the Sceptic being found to have contributed no helpful guidance toward our attaining to certainty, as to what we may believe, or not believe. While to submit to the dictation of the experts,—the old priestly dictation under another name—would be to surrender my intellectual independence; and that were intolerable to a Freethinker.

No: the only limitation that can be prescribed for our beliefs is, that no statement or inference shall be accepted as reliable, which is in manifest contradiction to any well authenticated principle or law directly bearing upon the matter submitted for belief. Beyond that, belief may have free range; being guided, of course, by good sense, and restrained from taking up with foolish notions, by large knowledge, and a wise discretion. Now I venture the affirmation, that there is not a sane "believer" within the compass of the Christian world who is not ready to admit, that wherever absolute, necessary contradiction can be shown to exist between any article of his creed and any law or principle certified by Sense or by Science, that *there* all talk about faith would be insufferably absurd. The faith of Christian men rests on *probable* evidence.

Faith may go whithersoever she will, then; or whithersoever any tolerably well-grounded evidence may justify her going. And it is something to be allowed to break away from the narrow creed of the Materialist. We may even go out 'mid the facts and phenomena of Christian history, gathering up data for beliefs—or which beget beliefs when gathered—from records of spiritual experiences, and from the social effects of the doctrine of Jesus; material thus accumulating on our hands for a tolerably complete orthodox creed; we finally accepting as credible, it maybe, "mysteries" from which Reason at first started back. But all this upon the supposition, of course, that we have jealously respected every law ruling in the constitution and course of things, natural or moral. "But we cannot believe in things unreasonable," it may be said. To which it might be replied that we certainly can, and do; being careful to mark the exact logical force of the word unreasonable; not clothing it with a *positive* force, as is so often carelessly done, but with a *privative* force simply; the word unreasonable meaning, when strictly taken, not what is *contrary* to Reason, but only that which Reason cannot as yet take in. The non-reasonableness, or the non-believableness, of a matter may rest on either of two grounds: either on the ground that belief in such matter would be in clear contradiction to some unquestionable truth; or the non-reasonableness may be simply temporal, or contingent—as when resting on, or rising out of, ignorance, as so often—which ignorance being dissipated by the incoming of larger knowledge touching the matter, that which was before unreasonable becomes reasonable; the domain of Reason being widened and her vision strengthened by such increase of light. For much of such increase of sphere and faculty, Reason has been indebted to Faith; Faith having often ventured forward beyond the boundaries of the known into the dark, so to speak; bringing back reports that have encouraged Reason to advance across the line till then deemed impassable; she so coming upon truths, at times, which she has adopted into her own creed; Faith being to Reason, in this connection, what hypothesis is so often to an advancing Science. Locke's oriental Prince scouted the statement of the Dutch ambassador, that water in his own country was sometimes so hard and strong that it would bear an elephant; the unreasonable for him resting upon uninformed experience. The work of Copernicus, with that of Galileo, startled the whole ecclesiastical world of the time to a frenzy of alarm and hate; that men should dare to deny the Divine Oracles, and to teach what was so outrageously contrary to the scientific decisions of the Church;—for the Church was then supposed to know, and to be competent to decide, everything, as being the organ of the Divine infallibility. But time passed on, and the rage of Church rulers died down; the mammoth mechanism of the heavens maintaining its serenely steadfast order, till the unreasonable became the reasonable, the incredible the credible!

Christian Faith is not the idle or simply sentimental thing, then, which some men so lightly, or so scornfully, assume it to be; but is as rational a power, in its place, as any that have to do with the conduct of moral life. Let the facts upon which it holds be shown to be no facts, but inventions, or superstitious conceits simply, and then men may smile at, or scoff at, the faith that should be so deluded. But as long as Christian men can produce as reliable reasons for belief of its principles and doctrines as can be shown in support of beliefs in the facts of secular history, or for the trust that men repose in the testimony of their fellows, not only is scoffing out of place, but the duty is imposed upon every man coming to a knowledge of those reasons, to put himself into a fair attitude of mind toward Christian evidences; that they may work in him whatever conviction of the truth of Christ's religion they may be capable of working. For the question is not between Faith and Sense, or between Faith and Demonstration, as Scepticism so generally states the case; but the question is: What kind and amount of pertinent proof, will warrant and require our trusting the alleged truths of Religion? And when the controversy between Faith and Unbelief assumes that shape, Faith is ready with her witnesses; with no fear of an adverse decision from those sitting in judgment. Bearing in mind always, however, that while the evidence for Christianity may be sufficient, it may not be exhaustive of all difficulty; nor always satisfactory to the Christian "believer." But we do not accept Christianity *because* of its intellectual difficulties, but *in spite* of them. There may arise occasions in the career of the most intrepid inquirer, indeed, when both Reason and Faith are brought to a stand; when a man can neither affirm nor deny as to some point at issue in debate; but a sensible man, when he has thus reached the end of his tether, will neither resent the limitations which the Creator has imposed upon his powers, nor say in a fit of anger,—Because I cannot know everything I will believe nothing.

Some of my readers will say, or feel, I suspect, that a very "low view" of Faith has prevailed throughout this discussion; but that is because I have been chiefly concerned to find a foothold for Faith in Reason. With that accomplished, our higher views of Faith may come in unquestioned. I know what is missed. Faith is an inspiration of the spiritual consciousness, as well as a formulated collection of opinions or dogmas. There is no conceivable limit to be prescribed to the power of Faith; when, having passed down from the head to the heart, so to speak, it seizes a man's deepest feelings, and gives new tone to his convictions, kindling his enthusiasms into glowing flame. For I don't believe in the artificial distinctions of the theologians as to various *kinds* of faith. The difference between a cold, formal faith, and a faith heroic or seraphic, is owing, very largely, to differences in the nature, and the varying degrees of importance, of the truths apprehended by faith; somewhat to differences in the constitutional capacity in men for intense feeling of any sort. In one man faith may assume the form of mere opinion,—if we may so degrade the word—while in another it may gather into the consistency of a conviction, while in a third it may kindle into a rapturous love; distinctively Christian faith having always a good deal of feeling in it; the intellectual element seeming wholly lost, at times, in the homage and trust of the heart for Him whom the Gospel sets forth as the great object of Faith; Christ being the centre upon which all Christian truth converges. Should it be said, that this is only a little fanatic mysticism thrown in as leaven for my rationalism, I might answer, that the man knows little of human nature who has not learned that it is rationalistic and mystical by turns; and that in a broad and profound religious experience, the influence of both will always be seen and felt.

It may seem a hard, complicate task to get at what religious people call "a knowledge of the truth," with the embarrassing entanglements round us, and the liabilities to go wrong before us, which in following the light of Reason we are sure to encounter. "Is it not easier," some shrinking soul may say, "to follow the advice of my priest; (or of my preacher) who tells me that it is safer to *believe* than to reason?" But believe what? The whole task which it was thought to evade is before a man, when once that question confronts him. No: we are not to be nursed into a strong healthy spiritual manhood by any such process. Reason may be thus put to sleep for a time, but on awaking it will resume its perplexing questionings. There are risks, no doubt, in seeking truth for ourselves; but they are not very serious, if only a right bent of moral purpose be in us. Nor is the task of *finding* half as difficult as timid souls are apt to imagine. For it is not *all* truth we are called to know before doubt can be laid; but only enough of truth to give a Christ-ward direction and inspiration to the affections and life. "The evidence for religion," says Bishop Butler, "is fully sufficient for all the purposes of probation, how far soever it may be from being satisfactory to the purposes of curiosity." Or as Pascal puts substantially the same thought:—"There is light enough for those whose sincere wish it is to see, and darkness enough to confound those of an opposite disposition." The folly of some who really desire to believe the truths of Religion, but fail to find quiet of mind, is seen in this: in their virtually stipulating, that every difficulty that troubles them shall be solved, and every mystery they encounter made plain, before they will enter the school of Christ. But men of sense and penetration as to these things are forward to confess, that in the sum of Christian *credenda* they find many things beyond their power to explain, or to comprehend. Enough for them that the unknown can never invalidate the known. Things insoluble seldom prove occasions of stumbling to men of a wise thoughtfulness; recollecting, as they are so frequently called to recollect, the limited range of the strongest human faculties, and the mists that so often envelope the higher attitudes of truth. Happily for all of us prone to doubt, faith in Jesus Christ is a matter of very much narrower dimensions than faith in all the theologies! The truth that saves is simple, said Matthew Arnold.[1] "Truth lies in a little compass, and narrow room. Vitals in religion are few," said Dr. Whichcote.[2] It is a blessed thing for a man to be able to say of crowds of claims put forth by our various orthodoxies:—About these things, or those things, or the other, I care little. For me they are matters of uncertain obligation. One may hold them, or dismiss them, as may please his fancy, or his taste; or according to the measure of respect he may deem it proper to show toward opinions, inferences, speculations, devout conceits, that have come down to us embalmed in the reverence of ages; but holding them, or dismissing them, the man is no better, and no worse, as a Christian. How much so-

---

[1] "*Literature and Dogma*," Chap. vi.

[2] Quoted by Principal Tullock in "*Rational Theology in the Seventeenth Century*," Vol. 2, p. 108.

ever they may affect his "standing" in the Church to which he may belong, they will count for very little when the final estimate is passed upon him.

Reason and Faith, then, these two:—have I prevailed upon any of my readers to revere them both as divine? If so, *est Deo gratia.* Let us listen wisely, prayerfully, patiently, to the two voices that tell of earthly and of heavenly things, and we may find that all seeming discord between the two dies; the two testimonies blending sweetly into one. Or the perfect concord may never be known here, since here we "know but in part"; but "when that which is perfect is come, then that which is in part shall be done away." Meanwhile, let us use all the faculties God has given us, whether of head or of heart, fearlessly, but humbly, in following after rest for our restlessness. Something may be done even now to such end, by large inquiry, by disciplined thought, by opening the mind to all revelations, come whence, or through whatever avenues, they may. But much more, perhaps, by a sweet simplicity, by tenderness, by devoutness, and by a childlike following of the light we have till God shall make it more.

III.

ON INSPIRATION AND INFALLIBILITY.

III.

ON INSPIRATION AND INFALLIBILITY.

INSPIRATION is a boldly metaphorical term: a term belonging to the dialect of poets rather than that of philosophers. It is a loose, fluid term, lending itself freely to writing or discourse which does not call for close definition, or for nice discrimination in use. The word means, literally, an *inbreathing* or a *breathing into;* being applied to designate any invasion of the human mind or heart by any strong, quickening, illuminating, or uplifting influence from without; poets, painters, orators, heroes, and others, being commonly spoken of as having been *inspired*, upon their having done or produced something that has moved men in numbers to an enthusiastic admiration; as if the achievement was too wonderful for a man to have accomplished of himself, simply.

Yet has this loose, metaphorical term been compelled to do service for centuries, in discussions of very difficult questions in history and philosophy; to which discussions only terms of a well-defined and an unvarying meaning would have been admitted, one might have supposed. But such a supposition had been foolish. No other terms were available to those engaging in such discussions than metaphorical terms. To convey any conception at all to men's minds of the action of the Spirit of God upon the human spirit, in the way of imparting knowledge, or of quickening it to a higher life, could only be done in parable, so to speak: through similitudes drawn from human proceedings and applied to proceedings assumed to be Divine. Hence the abounding anthropomorphisms that we have, and of necessity have, in Biblical accounts of God's communications to, and dealings with, men. But this necessity was sure to tempt men to a good deal of purely fanciful or fanatical speaking and writing, in their dealing with the question of Inspiration, whether claimed for men, or for Books.

Long before the Christian era, claims had been preferred by leaders among the Jewish people in behalf of certain writings of their ancient lawgivers and prophets, notably in behalf of those ascribed to Moses, to an exceptional character and value; in that they had come directly from Jehovah, the very words having been dictated by His Spirit, as the

Rabbis held; the writings so venerated being at length gathered up into the collection which we call the Old Testament; uncertainty prevailing, however, for a time, among the authorities, as to whether this or the other book, of less established note, should be admitted into the sacred "Canon" or Rule, as the collection came to be called. To this Jewish collection of "sacred books," was added, later on, another, when Christianity had produced a literature, which we call the New Testament; for which Christian Scribes asserted an authority equal to that which the Jew had asserted for his Mosaic Torah. Particularly was this high authority asserted for certain Biographies of Jesus that had come into circulation, as also for writings of some of the Apostles of Jesus; the two collections, the Hebrew and the Christian, coming several centuries after Christ, to make up our Bible as we have it to-day, substantially; all parts of which Christian disciples have been required to accept as infallible, because *inspired*.

But here we come at once upon the vagueness of our word Inspiration in this service. That the writers of the books of the Bible, or the men who chiefly speak in and through those books, were often inspired in the sense of having their minds penetrated and possessed by true, noble, holy thoughts, which inspirations moved them to utter themselves with a quickening, elevating, and morally wholesome effect upon the affections and consciences of men with whom they had to do, and of men of the many generations since, as it has fallen out;—to these claims nearly all men of an adequate moral discernment assent to-day, I take it; whatever may be their mental attitude toward other claims preferred for the Bible. But *that* sort or degree of faith in the inspiration of Scripture is not enough for our Christian Rabbis, of the severely "orthodox persuasion." A disciple in their schools, to attain good standing, must be prepared to say *how far* the inspiration extends; or, rather, must avow his belief in the declaration that it extends to every word and syllable in the manifold Volume. To secure an explicit confession to this effect, an adjective is appended, very commonly, by orthodox religious teachers, to the noun Inspiration,—"plenary," "verbal," "inerrant"; disciples being required to profess faith in the adjective as well as in the noun: to declare that the inspiration of the Bible is *full*, that is; or that it applies to and penetrates every *word* in the Book; or that no trace of *error* or mistake can be found in it. It is only just to say, that none of the great historic Churches have put forth this extreme pretension. The great Ecumenical creeds know nothing of it. Nor can we find it in any of the less important symbols of individual ecclesiastical Bodies. The Greek Church and the Latin Church are sober and modest in what they say bearing upon the question of the inspiration of Scripture; as is also the Anglican Church; as witness the Sixth Article of the celebrated XXXIX: "*Holy Scripture containeth all things necessary to salvation: so that whatsoever is not read therein, nor may be proved thereby, is not to be required of any man, that it should be believed as an article of the Faith.*" Not a word or a hint have we here, it will be observed, as to members of the Anglican communion being under any sort of obligation to hold that every word in our Bible is inspired; and that in the sense that every word was dictated to Prophet, or Evangelist, or Apostle, by the Spirit of God. But though the Churches have been thus reserved in shaping their formularies of Faith touching the question of Inspiration, it is notorious that their teachers and preachers, particularly those of various branches of our Protestantism, have gone to the greatest lengths of extravagance in their dealing with the question. As witness one of them: "The Bible is none other than the voice of Him that sitteth on the throne," says the Rev. Wm. J. Burgon, B. D.[1] "Every book of it, every chapter of it, every verse of it, every word of it, every syllable of it, every letter of it, is the direct utterance of the Most High." This bit of intemperate declamation does not reflect much credit upon the scholarship of the Anglican Clergy of the time; but it may nevertheless be taken as representing the prevailing teaching of the Christian Church, or of its ministers, down from the earliest times. There is very little in the New Testament that can be brought to the support of the notion of "verbal" inspiration; or of the claim that the Old Testament prophets were wholly passive under the influence of the Divine Spirit, in making known the mind of Almighty God to men. But in course of time, the veneration cherished for the writers both of the Old and New Testaments, or for the books which bore their names, attained to such heights, that every syllable going to make up the contents of the books was held to have come directly from Jehovah; the writers acting simply as amanuenses, or penmen, to note down what was given them by the dictation of the Holy Ghost. This was

[1] Fellow of Oriel Coll. Oxford. Sometime Gresham Lecturer in Divinity.

the estimate, indicated more or less explicitly in writings that have come down to us, in which all the great Church Fathers held the Sacred Scriptures. To them, lawgivers, prophets, Apostles, were merely passive organs of Divine revelations. The inspired man was the *lyre*, simply; the Spirit of God was the *plectrum* which drew the required sound from the lyre. The prophet, or apostle, was the *flute;* the Spirit was the *player* of the flute. Even the rational-minded Clement, of Alexandria, declares, that, under the influence of the Divine Logos, the human mind becomes like a harp in the hands of a player; Cyprian affirming that the Christian apostles were simply reeds, to whom the Holy Spirit dictated the things they were to speak or write. Some of the Christian Fathers manifestly sympathized with the notion of Philo, which he derived from the heathen, that the true prophet delivered his message while in a state of ecstasy, or mania; the proper action of his own mind being suspended for the time, or replaced by the inspiring presence in him of the Divine Logos. So that the believer in "verbal" inspiration of our own time, may find abundant support for his faith in the Church Fathers.[1]

---

[1] For confirmations and illustrations of all this, see Dr. Ladd's "*Doctrine of Sacred Scripture*," Vol 2, pp. 71-76.

But the authority of the Fathers is worth very little in explorations into these matters. They knew nothing, of course, of what we now mean by Criticism; while they had little or no opportunity for the exercise of whatever native critical faculty they may have possessed, in the way of searching examinations into the genuineness and authority of the Old Testament books. The canon was practically closed before Christ came: was formally and finally closed in the year 90, A. D. by a majority vote in a council of Palestinian Jewish Rabbis; which canon, or collection of books so accredited to be Divinely inspired, was received by the Christian Fathers on trust in the accumulated testimonies and traditions which had won for the books the high and solemn distinction. For the Church Fathers had little Hebrew at command, it would seem. What they did know of the Old Testament, from personal study, they knew through the Greek Version which we call the Septuagint; a translation of the Old Bible which had been made nearly three centuries before Christ for the benefit of Israelites dwelling in Greek-speaking countries. For these and other reasons the first Church Fathers were incapable of sitting in critical judgment upon claims put in in behalf of the Hebrew Scriptures as infallibly inspired;

equally, and in every component part. The early church authorities *had* to receive the Jewish sacred books upon faith in the work and word of the Jewish Scribes who had collected the books, and had discriminated between them and other claimants to a place in the canon; together with the incidental, general, and therefore vague, attestations of Jesus and His Apostles. The witness of Church Fathers in support of the claim that our Holy Scriptures are inspired throughout, down to every word and syllable; and that all parts of the vast miscellaneous Collection are *equally* inspired, and therefore of equal authority in the formation of opinion and in the direction of conduct;—as to these things the witness of Church Fathers is rather misleading than helpful; and is only to be cited in admonition of foolish handlings of the Word of God. It is proof of mental imbecility in the man who affirms, that because certain men became prominent at a very early period in ecclesiastical affairs, they must have been the more capable of entering into, and of wisely adjudicating, all the questions of which Christian Scholarship has been slowly attaining to some degree of mastery through a struggle of fifteen hundred years. The precise reverse of this is the truth. Church Fathers may be accepted as witnesses to facts coming under their own observation; but as to attainments fitting them for the work of critically scrutinizing the credentials of ancient writings, or of floating traditions, they not only had few, but their inheritances and circumstances precluded all possibility of their having any of any effective and lasting account. Not till the "new learning" had gone somewhat widely abroad over Western Christendom, was any attempt of consequence made to go back of the letter of Scripture as it was then received and taught, into a critical valuation of the text and teachings of our Sacred Books. And then came the first serious shock to the notion of "verbal" inspiration, with that of the absolute infallibility of all canonical Scriptures.

One might well marvel as to how this accrediting of Divine inspiration to every syllable in our Sacred Books found favor with men of intelligence and discernment in early times; but still more may one wonder as to how the notion has continued in favor in the Churches, 'mid the constantly increasing light that has been shed upon the Scriptures by a devout Scholarship, from the time of Erasmus down to our own. I have just been trying to indicate how the first Christians came to entertain the superstition. The belief in verbal inspiration was already in full possession of the Jewish religious mind; which belief Jesus and His Apostles seemed to have authenticated, by their references to, and citations from, the ancient Scriptures. It therefore passed without questioning into almost universal acceptance with the Primitive Church. Some early Christian writers found difficulty in retaining faith in the generally prevalent assumption. Origen, to wit, and Augustine, and even Jerome, who shows something like a fondness, indeed, for exposing the literary imperfections of St. Paul's writings.

But the Church Fathers did not suffer themselves to be very much troubled by the solecisms, or the contradictions, or the ethical incongruities which they came across in the Old Testament books. They had a way of escape which is not open to us in like straits. They had a twofold, or a threefold sense to fall back upon, in dealing with any passage that puzzled them. When a meaning which lay upon the surface of a passage did not suit them, or which seemed incredible, they had a *mystical* meaning ready; on the application of which all difficulty vanished. The time for criticism had not yet come; nor was it to come for long ages. But the other occasion for wonder that I just now named, cannot be so readily excused, or explained away. After frequent exposure of the untrustworthiness of the old traditional view of our Holy Scriptures; after serious difficulties have been pointed out which it needlessly imposes upon Christian believers; after it has been shown, again and again, in what unnecessary embarrassments the traditional view lands the apologist bent upon vindicating a rational respect and reverence for the Word of God; our spiritual guides, of the "evangelical" order, are still demanding that we believe in the dogma of verbal inspiration, or of the absolute infallibility of every syllable of our Bible! How the belief gained currency in the "reformed churches," so-called, admits of easy explanation. The assumption was accepted passively, or from an incurious piety, by our Protestant forefathers; just as the Rabbinic tradition had been accepted by the early Church Fathers. But in addition to this, there was a reason of peculiar force which favored its reception by the men who led in the revolt against the Romish hierarchy in the Sixteenth Century. Luther and his coadjutors had lost faith in an infallible *Church*, and they therefore took readily to trust in an infallible *Book;* which felt necessity of an infallible guide through all difficulties in or about Religion, and of an infallible arbiter in all controversies, and of a readily available and an unimpeachable rule of opinion and conduct, continues to lend good countenance to the assumption of verbal inspiration.

And yet, with the Scriptures open before us, opportunity being so afforded to all to "compare Scripture with Scripture", and with sufficient learning—once almost wholly the possession of professional scholars,—in the hands of the people to enable them to look into, and to understand somewhat of, these questions, it is really marvelous that the old orthodox dogma retains the credit it does. For when disciples are told that every word of the Bible is inspired, it cannot be meant that all the words of the various *versions*, or translations, of the Scriptures, or the words of any one of them, are to be so esteemed; for there are many hundreds of words in these versions in behalf of which no sane man would presume to prefer a claim to a special inspiration. Will it be preferred, then, in behalf of the ancient *manuscripts* of the Bible? or of any one of them?—the oldest and most complete? But what then should we do with the thousands upon thousands of *various readings* of these manuscripts? Who shall say which readings correctly and precisely represent the *ipsissima verba* which the

Spirit of God dictated to the original writers of our Biblical books? And what, moreover, of the interpolations that are found in the Sacred Volume? and of manifest mistakes of copyists? and of "emendations" made in the interests of "the Faith"? and of citations from Pagan writers? Those whom I am here trying to relieve of a groundless but very embarrassing prejudice, will not accept all these as coming up to the measure of their requirements. What, then, shall they do? for all these things are in their Bibles. It becomes obvious, that to satisfy the man who declares, in effect, that his faith will be undermined if you take away the comforting assurance that he has that every syllable in our Bible was dictated to this or the other writer by the Holy Ghost;—it is clear that to meet his case —and multitudes like it—we must recover the original *autographs* of the sacred writers. But that, alas! cannot be done; not even to save men or women from being bereft of "comforting" beliefs. Why don't the religious directors of these exacting people just hint to them, that the most they can fairly demand from Almighty God for their satisfaction in the shape of inspiration, is enough to guide them in the way of sound sensible believing, and of holy living. And it is not very extravagant praise to say, that the Bible *as it is* is abundantly sufficient for these things. But, unfortunately, the directors themselves stand most in need of the counsel just suggested; for the old traditional view has for sometime been slipping away from the hold of the members of our Churches whom we denominate "the laity"; this fatal objection to the conceit being obvious to "unlettered" readers of the Bible, that neither Jesus nor His Apostles attach any importance to mere *words* in their citations from the Old Testament Scriptures. It sufficed for them to give their hearers or readers the *sense* of this or the other passage they had occasion to quote from Moses or the Prophets.

But, dismissing the question of *verbal* inspiration, I proceed to submit objections to other orthodox views of the Bible, or of the Biblical writers. The presumption has prevailed that these writers were all *equally* inspired; and that *all which came from them* was alike inspired; so that wherever we may dip into the Bible we are sure to come upon utterances in the highest sense Divine and infallible. But these assumptions are even ludicrously silly. There has been an evolution in the method of Divine revelations to mankind. Light from Heaven did not come in full flood at first: it increased from dawn to day; such progress being traceable in the Record that we have of successive revelations. It were therefore foolish to claim that the Spiritual light vouchsafed to Moses, is equal to that which shone "in the face of Jesus Christ"; or that all the sayings attributed to Solomon, or to Psalmists, in the Old Testament, are of equal truth and authority with the sayings of St. John, or of St. Paul. Yet this claim is practically preferred by many of our preachers, as it is by multitudes of their disciples, as they plunge at random into the Bible; bringing out of it whatever may seem to suit them, or whatever may seem to support the dogma they are advocating; and all without question as to the real pertinency or the essential authority of the thing cited. Many sayings of the ancient Scriptures, and many customs, religious and political, which they enjoin, have been rendered obsolete for Christian people by the coming of Jesus Christ. This ought to be clear, even to children in our Sunday-schools; since a considerable portion of Christ's Sermon on the Mount, as we call it, is occupied in correcting the invalidated teachings of "the ancients"; among whom the traditional Moses is to be counted. While as to customs or institutions, those of us most given to swearing by the letter of Scripture, will not contend that human slavery and a plurality of wives ought to have been continued, because they were allowed by Jewish lawgivers and priests under alleged sanctions from Heaven. The popular religious view of this matter is blindly indiscriminating. The Song of Solomon is *not* of equal value with the Gospel of St. John, nor the Chronicles with the Acts of the Apostles. Truth as it is in Moses, or in the Prophets, must be judged by "truth as it is in Jesus." The Bible is *not* all of a piece. It is really humiliating that one should have occasion to emphasize so plain and obvious a truth to-day. But so it is. We Protestants have had the reputation of being readers and students of the Bible beyond all other religionists; but much of the reading has been dull, mechanical, or merely routine reading; with a latent assumption in the minds of most readers, that what was read was equally true and Divine; whether from the book of Judges, with its savage manners and morals; or from the Gospel according to St. Luke, with its story of the good Samaritan and its parable of the Prodigal Son. The theory that all Scripture is equally inspired, and of equal worth, is thus seen to be encumbered with difficulties which, being thoughtfully considered, ought to put its stoutest defenders out of all countenance.

They will not, upon reflection, contend, I am sure, that all the sentiments uttered in the fivefold or sixfold controversy carried on through the book of Job are from the dictation of Almighty God. The book of Psalms, again, is full of irreconcilable sentiments. Many of them are charged with the richest unction of the Spirit; but others of them are atrociously inhuman. At many of them devout-minded men and women shudder, often, as they hear them read out in our Churches. We have elaborate apologies in abundance for the "vindictive" Psalms; but they are all wasted. When the best apologetic arts have been tried, the vindictiveness—the almost fiendish vindictiveness, in some instances—remains. The unwelcome truth is clear, that men speaking in the name of God could in those days, as they can in these, get angry with their adversaries, invoking the most terrible calamities upon them; just as godly men have *burned* adversaries in crowds for the honor of the Lord Jesus Christ. And it is vain, I submit, it is blasphemous, to say that all these explosions of a cruel anger were inspired by the Spirit whose "*fruits are love, joy, peace, longsuffering, gentleness, goodness, fidelity*" (Galatians v. 22, 23). The varying and contradictory moods of mind, moreover, which we find reflected in the book of Ecclesiastes, cannot all be ascribed to the one source of unmixed and immutable Truth.

No: the Bible is not all of one piece. Those of us who hold that it is, are more densely superstitious in our estimate of Sacred Scriptures than the ancient Jewish Rabbis were; for they had their *three grades* of authority, at least, which they claimed for their Sacred Books; or their three degrees of inspiration. The highest place in their regard was occupied by the Law, or the five books of Moses; the next, lower, by the Prophets; the next, and lowest, by The Writings, or Holy Writings; (Hagiographa) most of the Rabbis ascribing a very uncertain amount of inspiration to these. But our orthodox Christian teachers, in their uncritical, clumsy estimates of the Scriptures, have grouped all the books, and all the writers, in one category of importance; to the confusion of many of their disciples, and to the very serious damage of the reputation of the Bible. One might have supposed, that some distinctive position would have been assigned by these teachers to Incarnate Wisdom. But nay: the Lord Jesus would seem to be no more to them than the man who maunders over the vanities of life in Ecclesiastes, or than the man who writes an epithalamium on the marriage of

Solomon to a heathen princess. (Psalm 45.) But more, along this line. The person inspired—this or the other of the sacred writers—is not *always and uniformly* inspired. Among men who have been so "moved by the Holy Ghost," we must surely count St. Paul; yet he himself tells us that he sometimes spake *of or from himself*, having no commandment from the Lord (1 Cor. vii. 6, 12); while, without such assurance, we can clearly perceive in certain passages of his Epistles that he is so speaking *from himself*—as in the weaving of that curious allegory about Abraham and Hagar, and the "two covenants"; where Paul manifestly falls into Rabbinizing, in a literary sense, of the most approved kind in the schools of the Scribes. Peter, again, in some respects the very chief of the Apostles, was not always constrained by Divine influence. He certainly *was* so constrained, in the main, when he wrote his letter to his brother Israelites of the Dispersion; but he certainly was *not*, when playing the Jew among "those of the circumcision," and the Christian among those who had renounced, and who denounced, circumcision—for which double dealing Paul rebuked him "to the face" (Galatians ii. 11–16). In which case, in this unhappy *rencontre* between the two Apostles, not both of them, surely could have been inspired by the good Spirit.

But are we not expressly told, some one of my readers may ask, that "*all* Scripture is given by inspiration of God"? We are; according to an inexact rendering of certain words of St. Paul in his second letter to Timothy, iii. 16. Correctly construed, however, the Apostle does not assert in the passage that all, or every, Scripture is inspired of God; but that *every Scripture so inspired is also* "*useful for doctrine, for reproof, for correction, for discipline unto righteousness.*" Even the very careful, and cautious, and abundantly competent Bishop Ellicott so renders. But even taken as our orthodox Scribes have been wont to take it, the passage could not be brought forward to guarantee the inspiration of the New Testament; since the Book was not written, or "published," at the time St. Paul wrote his letter to Timothy.

But it may be yet farther complained, that the old conventional view of Inspiration is a great deal *too narrow*. It is too narrow in respect of *time*, and it is too narrow in respect of *space*. It confines the enlightening and hallowing work of the Holy Spirit to certain periods of religious history; long since passed, and of very limited lengths compared with religious history as a whole. Men have presumed to assign beginnings and endings to the Spirit's work; in the sphere of Revelation, at least. It began with Abraham, say they; and ended—when? With Malachi? or with Ezra? or with the men of the Great Synagogue? "Yes," says the Biblically orthodox *Jew*, "with one or other of these." "But no," says the Biblically orthodox *Christian;* "the Spirit's enlightening work then ended *for awhile;* but it began again in the ministry of John the Baptist. Nay, earlier: at the birth of the Divine Infant. And it ended again— when? At the death of the latest lingerer here of Christ's Apostles? or with the close of the canon of New Testament writings? Let us hope not. Let us hope that not one of these guesses is correct. Let us rather say, that ever since there have been creatures with hearts and consciences in them on this globe, there has been a Divine Spirit at work upon such hearts and consciences; and that this Spirit will continue His work, without suspense, as long as the globe shall be tenanted with such creatures. Something of this faith would seem to have possession of the Christian world to-day; since we hear crowds of people in temples praying for, and singing about, a living Holy Spirit; but when the preacher comes to talk about the Bible, one might infer that the mission of the Spirit to the world had been closed somewhere about the middle of the Fourth Century; all the inspiration available to men since that time being bound up in Books! Yet the preacher's Bible speaks of Christian disciples having "an unction," an annointing, "from the Holy One"; and of a Spirit that should guide its subjects "into all truth"; and of epistles "written, not with ink, but with the Spirit of the living God; not upon tables of stone, but upon fleshly tables of the heart" (2 Cor. iii. 3). Let it not be suspected for a moment that I am here disparaging Book-revelations. Μὴ γένοιτο. I am simply trying to support the charge I just now made, that the conventional religious view of this question of Inspiration is altogether too contracted, too unpliant: to show that there was an inspiration going before the formulation of "canons," and which has continued to move men to high and holy thoughts and aims ever since the canons were "closed." I cherish the conceit, myself, that the world is in possession of sundry inspired books written this side of the dark ages; but none of them, probably, equally inspired touching God, and the human soul, and religion, and righteousness, and the life to come, with the writings of Hebrew prophets, or of Christian Apostles.

But the conventional view is too narrow, also, in respect of *space*. The inspiring Spirit moved men within the confines of Judaism, as it afterward moved men within the confines of Christendom; but not elsewhere, say our conventionalists. Moses, David, Isaiah, John, Paul, were inspired, say they; but Socrates, Sakya-muni, Marcus Aurelius, Dante, Shakespeare, were not inspired. But, accepting this narrow view of the Divine Spirit's operation in the world of moral intelligence and feeling, in what estimate are we to hold the lofty wisdom and the pure goodness which we revere in men who lived beyond the limits within which our orthodox teaching confines the gifts of Inspiration? Whence words like these? are they from heaven, or of men?—"A sacred Spirit dwells within us; the observer and guardian of all our evil and our good." "When the intellect is pure as well as the heart, to it the region of the Deity becomes visible." "God is near you, is with you, is within you." "Be self-denying, but do not boast of it: keep a watch upon yourself as your own most dangerous enemy. Do not plume yourself upon intellectual knowledge, which is in itself quite valueless, but upon a consistent nobleness. Never relax your efforts, but aim at perfection." "Bury my body as you please, but do not mourn as if you were burying Socrates. Think of me, rather, as gone to be with the wise and good; and with God, the fountain of all wisdom and goodness."[1] These voices come to us from out the old heathen world; but, judging them by their spirit and contents, they are as worthy to be counted divine as some of the sayings to be found in the book of "Canticles." "Rare flowers from the garden of Nature," evangelical sentiment calls these wise and devout utterances; but we may be bold to say of them, without irreverence,—"*All these worketh that one and the self-same Spirit; dividing to every man severally as He will.*" For St. Paul himself places precisely such an estimate upon certain utterances of Pagan wisdom which he cites. From his Helenistic training and associations at Tarsus, he had become acquainted with Greek writers, it would seem; which knowledge he does not disdain to use as a Christian Missionary, of which fact the record of his visit to Athens presents a striking instance. In the conduct of his great argument on Mars Hill, he accordingly quotes a line from the poet Aratus in support of the doctrine

[1] See Conway's "Sacred Anthology"; *passim.*

of the universal Fatherhood of God, for which he was contending. (Acts xvii. 28.) In his First Epistle to the Corinthians again, he gives us, approvingly, a sentiment from Menander: —"*Evil communications corrupt good manners*"; while in his letter to Titus, (i. 12) he refers to Epimenides as a "*prophet.*" Thus, words and sentiments from heathen authors have become part of what we hold to be supremely inspired Scripture, and are themselves therefore inspired; and that not in virtue of their being in the New Testament. The inspiration must have been in the words when they came from their Pagan authors: it did not come into them in the process of transcription, surely.

"We must therefore enlarge our conception of the sphere and function of Inspiration; and that under requirement of Bible authority and precedent. St. Paul being judge, other men than Hebrew prophets and Christian apostles have been 'moved by the Holy Ghost' to the utterance of divine and everlasting truth. Says Canon Farrar, in his admirable little book on *Seekers after God*—'God has spoken to men πολυμερῶς καὶ πολυτρόπως; at sundry times and in divers manners, with a richly variegated wisdom. Sometimes He has taught truth by the voice of Hebrew prophets; sometimes by the voice of Pagan philosophers; and all His voices demand our listening ear. If it was given to the Jew to speak with diviner insight and intenser power, it was given to the Gentile, also, to speak at times with a large and lofty utterance; and we may learn truth from men of alien lips and another tongue.' Doubtless, the highest and best results of the Spirit's work in and over men's minds and hearts have been gathered up, by a law of 'natural selection,' so to speak, into the Volume which we therefore hold to be inspired κατεξοχήν. Such honor cannot be claimed for it exclusively, however, but only as to excellence of degree. The Divine Father has been in living contact with men through other avenues of intercourse than book-revelations, and far beyond the limits of the Jewish and Christian Churches. The light supernal has, no doubt, shone most clearly in and through them; but human reason, too, has been a 'candle of the Lord'; the conscience has been a prophetic voice in the moral conduct of life; men 'doing by nature' the works of a law which they knew not otherwise than as written in their hearts. These, also, are among the 'fruits of the Spirit'; with all that is true and wholesome in art, in literature, in social order,—in civilization, in a word."[1] For

[1] "North American Review," Sept. 1884.

the artist, too, is an inspired man, according to our Bible. (Exodus xxxi. 1, 2, 3) And if the artist, every other man endowed with any "good and perfect gift."

On these accounts the popular conception of the range of the Holy Spirit's inspiration in and over men, must be declared to be too narrow. The prevailing Bibliolatry of Christendom resents every suggestion of an extension of the range, however. The time was, when great leaders and teachers in the Christian Church—such men as Justin and the Alexandrian Clement, notably—could speak of saints and sages of Pagan nations as having been illumined by "*the true light which lighteth every man that cometh into the world*"; while Luther might exercise his right of discrimination between the pure Word of God and parts of the Bible which he deemed of inferior value, and yet continue in credit with the orthodoxy of his time, and of the times since his day; but no man may be thus daring to-day, without exposing himself to the fiercest fires of ecclesiastical hate and persecution. Now, all this is passing strange, considering the immense advances which culture has made within a hundred years; the assumption being very generally entertained that culture must needs have a broadening, liberalizing effect upon men's minds, in every sphere of thought. The assumption is well-founded and just, even as appertaining to the sphere of theological thinking; but the liberalizing effect of culture in this sphere, seems to be almost wholly confined to the *students and scholars* in and about the Churches. These men know well enough, of course, that investigation and scholarship have made another thing of the Bible from what it was to people who used to assume that the Book had somehow come directly down from Heaven, complete and perfect down to every punctuation point; but this innocent notion has been but slightly disturbed, I suspect, in its hold upon the rank and file of church members.

It has thus come to pass that we have to-day two sets of *credenda* held, or tenable, in the religious world of our time: one set for the esoteric few; and the other, for the exoteric many. And this condition of things is taken to be natural, and necessary. The preachers, very generally, and nearly all our Sunday-school teachers, are inculcating one set of *credenda*, and our great Christian Scholars another; a state of things which I look upon as not only anomalous, but full of danger to the reputation and vigor of Christ's religion. For when those who have sat meekly under the old traditional teaching come to read and think for themselves, many of them discover that much of what they have been taught won't bear scrutinizing; and so, having no firm ground beneath their faith in the Bible when their belief in the untrustworthy things in the Book has been shaken, they, or many of them, fall away from Religion into one or other of our Infidelities; silent or declamatory as temperament may dispose.

But while our orthodox notion of Biblical inspiration is thus seen to be, on the one hand, too narrow, it is, on the other, a great deal *too wide;* in that it carries with it an assumption of an absolute *infallibility;* which appertains, it is alleged, to every word and act of the writers of our Sacred Books. And here again we marvel, more than before, how such an assumption could ever have found acceptance with readers of the Scriptures of any discernment; especially in the later Christian ages. The position is maintained to-day, however, in the face of the exposures that we have of the unsound science to be found in Scripture, and of chronological confusions, and of unreliable legendary narratives, which a devout Christian Scholarship has pointed out to us, or has certified for us;—in the face of these things we are still assured, that the salvation of our souls depends upon our believing in the unimpeachable veracity and infallibility of every syllable of the Old and New Testaments! Still is the alarmed exclamation of John Wesley echoed in our ears, or exclamations equally insensate,—"If we abandon belief in witchcraft, we might as well give up the Bible":—a very foolish saying of a very wise man. It is these weak, fanatical, imbecile things from the professional friends of the Bible, that are most effectually undermining its credit and influence among the people to-day. "And one shall say unto him, What are these wounds in thine hands? Then he shall answer, *Those with which I was wounded in the house of my friends*" (Zech. xiii. 6). That faith in Scriptures and in Churches has survived the follies and offences perpetrated through long centuries by their "friends," argues, to my mind, that there is something ineradicably good and Divine in Scriptures and in Churches; that there is in human nature a constitutional need of what Religion is supposed to do for men;—need of light to guide them on their way to the grave, and of grace to help them in their times of trouble. Otherwise, faith in Religion had surely been dissipated, or changed into scorn, long ere this.

Yet will it seem to some of my readers, I suspect, that I have myself been occupied thus far in this Essay in the work of undermining the credit of Holy Scripture. I am willing to risk the imputation, however; relying upon the reader's ability to perceive, that I have been seriously intent upon establishing confidence in all the essential facts and doctrines of Scripture; by clearing out of the way of the inquirer into the Bible's claims to respect and reverence, certain needless hindrances; so revealing, or leaving to be discovered, firmer footing for faith in "things which cannot be shaken." I have been simply counselling—putting my aim otherwise—that the Bible shall be read and interpreted with an honest and a duly enlightened *discrimination;* that sayings or sentiments that have come down to us from ignorant and superstitious ages, shall not be counted Divine and eternally true merely because they are found in a certain Record of those ages; that whatever may be discovered in the Book that a progressive knowledge, or a progressive spiritual insight and sensibility, has discredited, shall not be imposed upon men as inspired by a Spirit of truth and holiness; that deeds which are counted criminal in men, shall not be imputed to the wise and ever-righteous God at the requirement of any merely pious conceit; that whatever in Books or in Churches, in brief, is found to be contrary to "the mind that was in Christ," shall on that account be dismissed from among the things which a Christian man "ought to know and believe to his soul's health;" leaving *opinion* free to play about such matters, and to make of them what it can. *These* are the demands I have made, expressly or by implication, in the conduct of this discussion; nor are they very threatening, I take it, to faith in Divine Revelations. All of them being conceded, the Bible's claims to our veneration and love would remain what they were. Nay: the "wood, hay, and stubble" that have gathered about the foundations of God's Truth in the course of ages being removed, the impregnability of the foundations themselves would become the more manifest. Not a single moral commandment of the Almighty would be thus invalidated; not a precept of the Divine Directory would be thus deprived of its virtue; not one of its precious promises would be bereft of its comfort for the Christian heart. The Bible would remain what it was, essentially. All the great solid arguments which we now bring to the vindication of the inspiration and authority of Holy Scripture, would not only be as available then as now; but they would be allegeable with a double force, when we should be free from all calls to defend the indefensible. The submitting of any such arguments, at length, would be out of place here. Such kind of work did not fall within the scope of my intention, at least, on entering upon my present task. But let no light-minded person conclude, that belief in the Bible's inspiration and authority is to be looked for only in ignorant, credulous people to-day. Such conceits are widely abroad just now, but they are intolerably stupid. Christian priests and preachers have been largely instrumental in giving them currency, however.

Is it not time we had wholly done with this clumsy and mischievous handling of the Bible —so affording less occasion to unbelievers to blaspheme? Is it not about time that we ceased from preferring claims in behalf of the Book which it never prefers itself; laying up confusion for ourselves when the claims are discredited; as we have found so often? Is it not time that we should cease from making foolish and impertinent demands upon God's Word? and from reading into it our own groundless imaginings, or those of our theological party? Let us cease, also, from all jealousy of Criticism; allowing the largest and most searching inquiry into the origin and character of our Sacred Books; never fearing that the Gospel of Jesus Christ may be thereby imperilled. Traditional views of the Bible may have to yield to the demands of a larger knowledge than our theological forefathers had attained to; but the Church has made many such concessions already, without serious shock to the essentials of its Faith. The earth is no longer the centre of the universe, but Christ is still the centre of the world's dearest affections and hopes. God's Truth was not given to men to satisfy the curious, or to silence the caviller, or to meet all the requirements of the critic. Going to the Holy Book with such expectations in us, we shall probably come away disappointed. No: the Scriptures were given us for "*instruction in righteousness; that the man of God may be thoroughly furnished unto all good works.*" Taking our stand on this ground, accepting the Bible as a guide to Christian believing and living, we may live at peace 'mid all the intellectual tumult of the time.

IV.
ON THE RACKING DOUBT.

IV.

ON THE RACKING DOUBT.

"*Who knoweth whether the spirit of man goeth upward, or whether the spirit of the beast goeth downward to the earth?*" is a question traditionally ascribed to Solomon; (Ecclesiastes iii. 21).[1] "Spirit" being credited to *beasts* by this Hebrew "wise man," the reader will note; which we moderns are inclined to do more and more, as we learn more and more of the higher orders of the animal kingdom.

The man who put the double question I am for the moment dealing with, had obviously no positive hope of a future beyond death for either beast or man. Both might go "downward to the earth"; which, to him, would be the end of both, we must infer. The going "*upward*" does seem to hint, however, at the possible existence of another state of being for man, on his passing out of this. Meanwhile this "Koheleth"—Preacher, Teacher, Wise

[1] No Biblical Scholar of our own time, however, holds that the Book of Ecclesiastes was written by the son and successor of David.
The translation is that of the "Revised Version."

Man—is in a state of sore perplexity; inclining at one time to yield to the suggestion that the end of man is in nowise better than that of the brute, since "*both go to the same place,*" as he goes on to tell us. But he seems to have emerged out of this confusion of thought and feeling, in part, at least; finally summing up the matter thus:—"*Fear God, and keep His commandments; for this is the whole duty of man.*"

Yet is there nothing very hopeful as to a future life in this. Our "wise man" tells us to be true to all the relations and obligations of the present; which is a good "working creed"; a creed in which men are more and more inclined to take refuge, I suspect, 'mid the darkling doubts of our time; but a creed of very little service to the man who persists in pushing the inquiry,—"Is all this doing of duty here to have any issues after death?" "Morality, the keeping of God's commandments, I acknowledge to be a substantial good," such a man might go on to say; "holding as I do, that whether men are to survive the grave or not, they are bound to do right, here and now, apart from all motives looking to another world for reward; the doing good only 'for the sake of eternal happiness' being a base principle of action, to my own moral apprehension." And the sentiment is just. It is a reckless thing to say, as some Christian teachers have said, in effect, that but for the fear of hell and the hope of heaven, they would make the best of this world upon any terms; even terms that might now be counted dishonorable.

Few men are satisfied, however, with the notion that this world is a place for work and pleasure solely; or with the philosophy which tells us to be content with the wages and the pastime we get here, and to lie down at life's close with no craving for anything beyond. To most of us, spite of our modern Epicureanisms, the old questions will recur, as we forecast the future—" What am I? Whither am I going, if anywhere beyond the limit of time so rapidly closing in upon me? Is the break with life to be final for me, when the pulse shall cease to beat? I fear it is; since so many learned tongues are telling me that so it is to be, for me, and for all; Science having resolved the doubt that plagued Solomon, as I am assured; in having proved that the old orthodox distinction between man and the brute was merely imaginary, or that the only difference between them is simply in the complexity of the cranial organization; the 'spirit,' or breath, which animates both, being destined to evaporate into the common air about us when the end for each shall come."

But Science has proved no such thing. Whether or not a better destiny be in reserve for man than for the brute hereafter, he is certainly in a more hopeful condition than the mere animal, for the time, or in the state, now present. In that he is capable of *a progressive education*, for instance.

> "Brutes soon their zenith gain: their little all
> Flows in at once. . . . Were man to live
> A thousand years, the patriarch pupil would
> Be learning still; and, dying, leave his lesson
> half unlearned."

Even so; men of the best and most thoroughly developed faculties, and of the widest and highest attainments, go forth out of this world with "germs of power in them which the influences of time have scarcely quickened into life"; and with aspirations after a knowledge of things of which they had been dreaming through all their career upon earth. But the brute has no intellectual germs to be further developed, here or hereafter, that we can detect. For the mere animal there are no arrested lines of inquiry to be taken up again after death, should opportunity be afforded. Let not the reader understand me as saying here, that the lower animals are wholly void of intelligence. We know better. We always did; but we disguised the fact by calling intelligence in creatures beneath us "instinct." What I mean to say is, that the merely animal intelligence is a fixed quantity, so to speak, not admitting of any very considerable increase or development. It is about to-day what it has been down from the farthest point in the past to which Natural History has carried its researches; nor is there any good likelihood that it will ever be very much more than it is now. Animal intelligence works ever upon the same fixed lines, about; producing ever about the same results. But in respect of the human intelligence it is conspicuously otherwise, as we all know. To its growth or expansion no conceivable limit can be assigned; the human mind having in it a capability of what may be deemed an endless development. On which ground one might predict a future life for man, while denying it to the brute.

To the support of which conclusion this familiar fact might be cited: viz, the illimitable and irrepressible aspirations to which the human mind is subject, of which we see little or nothing in the merely animal mind. Hence the stimulating discontent with their allotments or with their attainments observable in men, even in the best conditioned. Whatever a man may have of this world's good, he has ever a higher ideal before him, unless he be irredeemably dull. He conceives of, and he longs for, probably, conditions more desirable than those about him, coveting a good more completely satisfying than he has ever as yet known.

> "We love, and we long with an infinite greed,
>   For a love that will fill our deep longing in vain.
> The cup that we drink of is pleasant, indeed;
>   But it holds but a drop of the heavenly rain."

Which inappeasable instinct has suggested the inference, that we are destined for a state of being in which the yearning shall be satisfied. So have our spiritual instructors argued, at least.

No conclusive force is claimed for these hints and inferences, as bearing upon the question discussed in this Essay; but something more remains to be said.

"No conclusive force is claimed, indeed!" retorts the Agnostic.[1] "No, I should think

[1] This word was born, so to speak, only a few years ago. The occasion of its formal adoption into the dialect of British philosophy, at least, was at a meeting of a number of English *savants* at Clapham, near London, in the year 1869; the word Agnostic being then suggested—by Mr. Huxley, it has been said—as a fitter and a fairer designation than

ON THE RACKING DOUBT. 115

not. They are simply of the sort that have mystified credulous people for ages:—mere gropings in the dark, attempts to explain the inexplicable, to get at a knowledge of the unknowable, to make good at the bar of Reason doctrines that are beyond the reach of reason. Let, therefore, this beating of the old straw cease. Of any posthumous destiny for man we know nothing, nor did the wisest of our species in past ages know anything. It is vain, therefore, to betake one's self to prophets or oracles of any sort, in quest after a solution of the great enigma. We know phenomena only. Or, more correctly, all our knowledge is of states of consciousness simply." Well; the protest is vigorously put ; yet might one make answer that "gropings in the dark" have often led to light. While it might be said further, to the credit of free thinking, that, as a matter of fact, no line of inquiry into the constitution, or processes, or sequences of things, has ever

atheist, or infidel, of the men who refuse to accept the doctrines of our orthodox religionisms; such terms having gathered about them a certain amount of social odium, of which "freethinkers" don't deem themselves deserving. From that year—'69, therefore, the word Agnosticism has been made to do service as a mild and inoffensive substitute for the term infidelity. Men who reject doctrinal Christianity, are no longer to be called infidels, but are to be known and spoken of as Agnostics. And I for one, would cheerfully allow the substitute; the request for the change being, in my judgment, reasonable and fair.

been arrested for long by any dictum of authority. Told that fuller knowledge was not to be found on the path of investigation they were pursuing, inquirers have surmised that the lack of knowledge might be only temporal; and have gone on with their inquiries. And it were vain for the agnostic to expect that his dictum will prove a whit more effectual, in the way of silencing the "whence," "why," "whither," which each generation of men puts with unwaning eagerness, on attaining to intellectual puberty—our own not less eagerly than the generations that are gone. Spite of the very marked devotion to physical studies that has prevailed throughout the century just closing, questions of a psychological interest are as widely and as intensely pondered to-day, probably, as in any past period of intellectual history; all the more intensely from recent psychical researches of which the world has heard. With certainty may it be said, that a philosophy which rudely shuts the door in the face of inquirers into questions of such moment as the higher endowments of men, and their possibly everlasting destinies, saying "There is no light to be had here," will fail to win to itself a very wide and warm attachment in this our free-thinking age. For here, at least, *Christian* thinkers claim to be free thinkers.

From all this it will be clear, I trust, that I myself cherish no enmity toward, or fear of, Agnosticism. Touching many things, powers, functions, seen and unseen, in the vast, manifold, mysterious whole of which we ourselves are parts, we are all agnostics. My objection to considerable parts of our theological "systems" is, that they are a great deal *too knowing;* theologians having been long accustomed to talk in a shockingly familiar way about what they nevertheless call "the deep things of God"; as if all the secrets of the hidden world were naked and open to them. They can tell one all, or very much, about what they call "the counsels of eternity"; as though they themselves had been present at the high council board, and had well understood all that was considered and decided there. They know, or they assume to know, also, all the underlying reasons of the things that have been, and that are, and that shall be; with all the ultimate purposes of the vast scheme of Providence, which unrolls itself so slowly and so perplexingly in the process of the ages. The courageous theologian will even analyze the nature of the ineffable Godhead for you; actual specimens of which daring work we have in the so-called "Athanasian Creed," and in many of our treatises upon the doctrine of the Trinity. But all that sort of thing is intolerably offensive, to men of discernment and modest feeling; who know well the very limited range of the strongest intellectual faculties, in dealing with matters beyond the direct cognizance of the logical understanding. As to these things we are all, in large part, at least, agnostics, or ignorant ones.

But are we quite and as inevitably ignorant of the higher truths of Religion, or are we as completely destitute of all good ground for belief in them—in the doctrine of a Future Life, for instance—as our agnostics would have it that we are? "Yes," we are answered, with emphasis :—"Yes: we are all thus absolutely ignorant, the Christian sophist included, of what he calls 'the higher truths of religion.' We know only *phenomena*." Indeed! we say on recovering breath; adding, perhaps, the inquiry :—And is the case—this whole controversy between materialism and spiritualism—to be thus easily and neatly disposed of? And all by simply citing a vague or an unmeaning verbal formula? But in that case,—all our knowledge being of phenomena only, that is, —how much of what we have hitherto been accustomed to call knowledge must be dismissed from such high regard! All the vast stores of history, for instance; with all that world-wide travel tells us;—of these we are no longer to be said to know anything. For though the incidents, events, transactions of which the historian or the traveler informs us may have been phenomena *to him*, they have certainly not been phenomena to men living in later ages; or to men who were living *at the time* in other parts of the earth. *They*, therefore, cannot be said to have known such events or transactions. Yet have men for ages been under the delusion, that from pondering the pages of Thucydides, or Livy, or Hume, they have come to *know* something of what Greeks, or Romans, or Englishmen actually said and did in those times. But let all this go. It is simply a question of using the word "know" with, or without, a special emphasis. This very considerable thing may be here added, however, that in no other sense can we be said to know the agnostic's phenomena, than that in which we may be said to know history; *this* knowing, and *that*, resting on, or being got at, by *faith*.

I should be willing, myself, to accept the agnostic's short, bold, blunt declaration—"We know only phenomena," provided it should be understood that *all* phenomena were to be included within the scope of the formula's meaning or intent; not only *objective*, but *subjective*, phenomena :—thought, feeling, desire, will, intuition, the logical instinct, the faculty of generalization—*all* mental phenomena, in brief. I should insist upon this stipulation for the purpose of precluding all possibility of its being concluded, that we know nothing beyond impressions made upon the cognitive faculties by *sensible things;* a conclusion which the less cautious of our agnostic scribes tempt their readers to run away with, by the unqualified, headlong way in which they deliver themselves of what they have to say. All that sense does not affirm, or that science does not demonstrate, say they, is to be relegated to the sphere of poetry, or sentiment, or faith,—for which agnostics have but small respect. It is all superlative nonsense, however. Yet will this jingling of verbal formulæ still go on, probably, in college lecture-rooms, and in "halls of science." It would be very disorderly, but it might prove of service, should some one of the disciples rise in his place and say—"Sirs: suppose that, passing on from connoting *appearances*, we start in quest of *realities;* asking—Of what are appearances the appearances ? and—To what, if anything, do appearances appear?" Such a disciple would be rebuked, of course; and might be told, that such questions are out of place in the lecture-room of a teacher of Physical Science; the reminder being added, possibly, that it is for the *Metaphysician* to do what he can with such questions: as for Physicists, they no longer trouble themselves with "extinct follies." Yet would the neophyte who should be thus daring, be on a true intellectual scent: a scent which even the Physicist will have to follow, to get at the real meaning of his phenomena.

But let all this go, I say again—all this talk as to sensible phenomena being the limit of all possible human knowledge—as being of very little consequence, one way or other. It is, in truth, of no consequence whatever; as we may perceive very clearly on recurring to the alternate formula offered us a little while ago by the agnostic. "All our knowledge is of *states of consciousness*," he then told us; and to this all Rabbis eminent in the schools of agnosticism to-day agree; which is a decided advance toward clearer thinking about this whole matter. All that I bargained for, then, or which I threatened to demand, should the discussion of the old formula be seriously entered upon, has been conceded. The field of debate has been very much narrowed. We have no longer *two* classes of phenomena to distract our attention—the objective and subjective. We have only *one* class to do with now—the *subjective;* for all our knowledge is of *states of consciousness,* simply, and wholly; for the unquestioned adoption of which formula, all believers in what we call the "soul," and in the possibility of souls surviving death, may well be thankful.

The appeal now lies to Consciousness, then; or to the mind, soul, spirit: to its sense of Self; to its susceptibilities, capabilities, and to its actual workings; to thought, feeling, intuition; to its reflections and anticipations; to its instinctive discriminations; to its "categoric imperatives"; to its shame for, and detestation of, knowingly-done wrong. These are the phenomena we shall have to do with for awhile. And these we certainly *know*—using the word with the full pressure of the required emphasis upon it—and none other, properly speaking.

Consciousness is an ultimate fact in human experience; so simple and direct in its nature and witness that we cannot define it, as Sir William Hamilton remarks. I know that I know; I know that I feel; I know that I desire—that is all there is to be said about the matter. While the phenomena of consciousness are so uniform and of so unvarying a significance to all sane natures, as they have been among all civilized peoples in all ages, that we receive them, and swear by them, *nemine contradicente*.

But in what way can the witness of consciousness help us to a rational and reliable *belief* in a future life? For I am not here bent upon *proving*, in the sense of demonstrating, that men will live after death. We have no argumentative materials at command for the accomplishing of that task. The posthumous life of which we conceive, is beyond the apprehension of the senses—"*Eye hath not seen*"; and as to ghosts, we cannot bring them into court in the trial of this case. I aim at nothing more in this Essay, at least, than to make sufficient ground good for the resting of a belief upon it, that what we call the "animating principle" in us, the life force, of which we are now conscious, *may*, not assuredly *will*, survive the dissolution of the body; so far meeting and refuting the dogmas of our Materialism. To such extent, or toward the attainment of this aim, the responses of Consciousness to our appeal will be found helpful, I anticipate.

The brain is the organ of the mind, if it be

still permitted us so to speak; which organ the Craniologist dismembers, and proceeds to distribute into a variety of quasi-independent organs, a special function being assigned to each; the matter filling *this* recess in the cranium being perpetually busy in producing the sentiment of awe; the matter in *another* recess producing benevolent emotions; while other matter so located shows a passion for destructiveness; still other "organs" showing pitifulness; and so on with other cranial protuberances, or recesses; the brain, in its structure and functions, being thus seen to be *manifold;* as interpreted by the Phrenologist. But Consciousness testifies that the mind is *one*, not many. Back of, or beneath, all diversity of organs is the necessary Unity of the thinking, feeling, acting Agent. For it is the same Something which feels, and reasons, and which shapes conceptions of beauty; which throbs with animal passion, and which is inspired with sympathy and love. All these are faculties, affections, energies, not of the individual organs to which they are loosely accredited, but of the *Ego;* of the Soul, of the Spirit, of the Man; who *owns* the organs, so to speak; and operates through them, as through the keys or stops of some musical instrument. The music is *varied*, but the Player is *one*.

ON THE RACKING DOUBT.

By few mental scientists is the cranial map-work of the Phrenologist accepted, however, as usually presented; but they, too, dismember the Mind, by *personifying* its powers; labeling them as perception, reason, judgment, affection, desire, will; these capabilities being represented by writers in this field, as severally *doing* or *suffering* this or the other thing;—*each on its own account*, so to put the point. This is not *meant* of course, by the writers. It were well for readers to recollect themselves occasionally, however; clearly defining the truth to their thoughts, that such a way of speaking of the mind's susceptibilities and activities is after the manner of the poet, rather than that of the philosopher. For it is not the judgment that judges, or desire that desires, or the will that wills; but it is the one all-inclusive Mind, or Soul, that judges, or desires, or wills. Yet is the poetical way of speaking, even of these high serious matters, quite allowable; nay, inevitable. Only, we are to discriminate; remembering always, or recollecting occasionally, that all organs and functions are the organs and functions of the *one Mind*.

We have thus come upon a conscious *Unity*, then, beneath the varieties of organ and of function appertaining to the human brain; to which Unity all sensations report themselves, and by which they are interpreted and classified. How the report is made, and how it is deciphered, and as to how an external form is translated into a mental image, and awakens mental emotion,—as to these things we know very little. We trace a sensation along an afferent nerve that is carrying it to the sensorium, till we lose sight of it, so to speak, 'mid the convolutions of the sensory ganglia. But it does not then cease *to be*. Consciousness receives it; retaining it, usually, for awhile. But either at once, or at length, it, or a weaker reflex of it, is stored away in the archives of Memory for future recall; should occasion ever incite the mind to recollection of it. Without a conscious Subject, however, there never could be a sensation, either to be recollected, or to be taken in.

But on following another line of observation we come upon this same conscious Unity again. The atoms constituting our physical structure are in continual flux, we are told by our physiological authorities; constituent elements being incessantly cast off out of the structure, and others being continually taken up into it, to supply the voids so created; the whole of our bodily organism, including the brain, of course, being renewed every seven years, or thereabouts. But the Ego, the Soul, our true Self, remains absolutely unchanged through the whole process of transmutation; retaining a cleanly cut sense of its Identity throughout. Now, in whatever this sense of identity may inhere, it certainly does not inhere, it may be confidently affirmed, in any collocation of material particles; for how could such particles be continually dropping out of our bodily frame-work, the sense of our personality remaining without the slightest variation or abatement? "All human language, all human observation implies," says one of England's acutest writers—himself a "freethinker,"[1] "that the mind, the I, is a thing in itself, a fixed point in the midst of a world of change; of which world of change its own organs form a part. It is the same yesterday, to-day, and to-morrow. It was what it is when its organs were of a different shape, and consisted of different matter from their present shape and matter. While it will be what it is when they have gone through other changes. I do not say that this proves, but it surely suggests, it renders probable, the belief that this ultimate fact, this starting-point of all knowledge, thought, feeling, and language, this 'final inexplicability,' is independent of its

---

[1] James Fitzjames Stephen, Q. C., in "Liberty, Equality, and Fraternity," p. 296, Am. Ed.

organs; that it may have existed before they were collected out of the elements, and may continue to exist after they are dissolved into the elements."

Spite of the perpetual flux of the atoms which constitute the instrument through which it usually acts, then, and spite of the variety of organs into which that instrument is distributed, the Mind is *one:* permanently and immutably *one.* But it remains one, also, through all the transitory stages it passes through in the course of its unfolding and maturing. If our experiences ran through the mind like water through a water-wheel, leaving no abiding impressions behind it, the past of a man's life would be a blank. But it does not so run away. It leaves deposits behind it, so to speak, which become parts of a man's self; so that all the past lives in the present, or *the man*, rather, lives in the past, in the present, and in the future: in the past by reflection, in the present by experience, and in the future by anticipation.

We are thoughtlessly familiar with the workings of Memory, or they might start a thousand curious questions in us very perplexing to materialism. How are its records written and preserved? On material tablets, and in material archives? Why, there is not room for them if the record ran round every particle in our physical constitution. How, moreover, could one constituent atom hand on its inscription, on leaving its place in the human organism, to its successor? If the Mind is only a congeries of material organs,—"secreting thought as the liver secretes bile"—however did it acquire its wonderful power of looking back, and of retaining impressions made upon it in remotely by-gone times? Or how does it exercise its forward-looking capability? Sense cannot take discriminating cognizance of things that have no existence except to faith, or to the imagination. But the Mind holds communion, familiarly and habitually, as we know, with experiences and associations of a far past through Memory. In hours of silent thought, all the senses being shut, the investiture of the body having seemingly fallen away from us, we relive our days and years; incidents of our youth being as real to the eye of reflection, up to advanced years, as the incidents of the present passing hour. The unworthy deed, the malicious word, the selfish feeling, comes back to us, crimsoning the cheek with a blush of shame, or moistening the eye with penitential tears, or smiting the conscience with a guilty fear, it may be. Or, if the word, deed, feeling, were true and good, filling the soul with a pleasant satisfaction when remembered; all which are strange susceptibilities and powers to attribute to a collocation of material particles, I take it.

But here I pass to considerations of an equal or even weightier significance in support of the thesis I am maintaining. Consciousness testifies to a capability of *moral Freedom* in men; a claim which is practically acknowledged by all men, though professedly denied by some. I do not allege, or assume, that this freedom is absolute or unlimited in us. It is restrained or hedged in by conditions, internal and external; freedom being of very limited possibility of range in some men, and of comparatively wide possibility of range in others; but in all it is conditioned. With endowment of the necessary faculties of mind, however, we are free to shape, not always to originate, our own purposes, and to follow our own preferences, within our own proper limits. Attempts have been made to refute this claim, or to deprive of all force arguments preferred in support of it. Mr. Tyndall, for instance, once told us, that there is an invariable relation between physics and consciousness, so that, "given the state of the brain, the corresponding thought or feeling may be inferred.

Or given the thought or feeling, and the corresponding state of the brain may be inferred"; in which statement Christian philosophy finds nothing to object to; since it only affirms the intimate connection which we know to exist between the mind and the instrument through which it ordinarily acts. Should any one be tempted, however, to conclude from the affirmation that a certain disposition of brain molecules *produces*, properly speaking, states of consciousness which have inevitable issues in conduct; and that therefore man is not free, being wholly under the inspiration and control of molecular action, the eminent scientist will supply such an one with a correction, where he says:—"You cannot satisfy the human understanding in its demand for logical continuity between molecular processes and the phenomena of consciousness. This is a rock on which materialism must inevitably split, whenever it pretends to be a complete philosophy of the human mind."[1]

Others have alleged, again, that the mind, and therefore life, is under the irresistible coercion of *Motives ;* a motive being assumed to be a something which moves the Mind, as the word imports; so moving the *man* to any line of action he may enter upon and follow;

[1] "*Fragments of Science,*" Introduction to Part II.

all this being taken as an adequate basis for the inference, that men being so constrained, —constrained by motives which they themselves do not invent, but to which they are wholly passive, as assumed—from all this it is argued that men are not accountable for their conduct, because not free to do what they would. But, in truth, a motive is simply a state of consciousness: an attitude of mind incited by some offer of gain or gratification, or by some other inducement to action; the decision of the question as to whether the offer shall be accepted, or the inducement yielded to, *remaining with the Mind itself;* what we call the "stronger" motive, in our popular loose way of talking, being only known to be "stronger" *after* the Mind has decided to do *this* with the offer, and not *that*. It is not true, therefore, to say that motives coerce the Mind. It would be nearer the truth, at least, to say that the Mind coerces motives.

Still others have affirmed that character and conduct are decided by inheritances from progenitors, and by the pressure of environment—using the word in a very wide sense—upon our nature; specially in its early pliant stages of development; according to an old but now disused formula—"Man is the creature of circumstances." All possibility of moral freedom for man is thus excluded again, therefore.

All these, however, with the conceit of "an eternally impressed series of consequences," are ineffectual attempts to get round the truth to which consciousness and experience testify: the truth of the Mind's spontaneity, of its power to strike the balance between claims submitted to it; which we see continually illustrated and confirmed, not by men of any particular school or creed only, but by men of all schools and creeds, in the free outflowing of their natures. Some men talk the talk of fatalism; but in pondering and fighting our way through the world we are all free men. If the Mind were not free to deliberate and to decide upon this or the other line of action, then could no sense or suspicion of accountability ever arise within us in the use of its powers and privileges; nor any feeling of remorse follow upon their abuse. But we *have* such a sense within us: such a feeling *does* follow wilful and deliberate wrongdoing. Man is morally free, then, within a varying circumference of action, or possibility of action; *or Consciousness lies.* Certainly, no conceivable combination of material particles could ever result in any but a mechanical, and therefore non-accountable, activity. The assumptions of Materialism are here wholly at fault, then; as by this time begins to be clear, I may conclude.

But let the reader take into consideration another fact, or series of facts, in mental experiences, of like import to those I have already adduced. The phenomena of "Unconscious Cerebration" suffice to show that the human Mind can act, even now, independently of the bodily organism; or, speaking more precisely, can act without prompting by the senses. That may be deemed a daring saying; but there is ample evidence to confirm its credibility, if we only knew what the evidence meant, or what it implied.[1] I retire at night, wearied with wrestlings at an insolvable problem. But in the night-watches, when all our faculties are asleep, as we are wont to think, the Mind has gone on with the task and completed it; the problem standing out to my apprehension on waking in the morning, cleanly solved. Or I have a project before me of a journey, with business at the end that absorbs me in anticipation. While I sit pondering my plans,

---

[1] "Experience furnishes us with no example of any series of states of consciousness, without this group of contingent sensations attached to it; but it is as easy to imagine such a series of states without, as with, this accompaniment; and we know of no reason in the nature of things against the possibility of its being so disjoined." John Stewart Mill, in his Essay on "*Immortality.*"

there is animated noisy intercourse going on all around me; but to me it is all as if it were not. I am not in the world of my actual surroundings. I am far away from it all, in a world of my own: in a world which has no existence, as yet, except to faith; in *a world of the Mind's own creating out of nothing!* The "molecular activities" have been all in full play the while, I am to suppose; carrying reports to the sensorium of the noisy sayings and doings about me, but I have been wholly unaware of them! It is all very strange, but such experiences are familiar. Yes: we are often looking with the eye when we do not see. The ear is often open when we do not hear. Every nerve may be in tune, and on full stretch, when we feel no sense of touch.

To these hints the reader will probably be ready to respond approvingly, saying within himself—"Yes; I have been aware of such things a hundred times in the course of my experience." Even so. And the explanation we give of them in our common talk, is profoundly just and philosophic, I believe. We ascribe such failures of apprehension to mental pre-occupation, or to what we call "absence of mind." Yes; that is the phrase which indicates the true account to be given of such phenomena. Just as the operator may be absent from the instrument when a message comes through a wire connecting two continents, perhaps, as a nerve connects the hand with the brain, such message remaining unread till the operator returns to his post; even so may the apparatus of the senses carry a report to the seat of intelligence, but it remains *unread* as long as the Mind is absent, or otherwise occupied. While we have all had experiences of similar import, in dim, mysterious reminiscences of a life lived by us in some past period of time, or in some other state of being. Yes; there come to us, we know not how, we know not whence, strange

> "Mystic gleams,
> Like glimpses of forgotten dreams:
> Of something felt, like something here;
> Of something done we know not where;
> Such as no language may declare."

Yet is the author of "*Intimations of Immortality*" bold to "declare," adopting Plato's conceit, that these "gleams" are distant reflections of a pre-earthly existence.

> "Our birth is but a sleep and a forgetting:
> The soul that rises with us, our life's Star,
> Hath had elsewhere its setting,
> And cometh from afar:
> Not in entire forgetfulness,
> And not in utter nakedness;
> But trailing clouds of glory do we come
> From God, who is our home."

But what is the Something which works these wonders within us? which sets all the known capabilities of matter at defiance? which ignores the limitations of Time and Space, making the past and the future present, and the non-existent actual? That Something is personal; for it calls itself "I." It is intelligent; for it writes Iliads, and elaborates Philosophies. It is free; for it deliberates and chooses; accepting this, and rejecting that. It is moral; for it condemns wrong, even its own wrong, and approves right. It is devout; for it worships.

Aye; says the unmitigated Materialist, but all these are the results of the inter-activities of material molecules, simply. Well; if they are, we shall have to discharge the old verbal dualism from further service; and learn to speak of Mind in terms of Matter, or of Matter in terms of Mind. But a new terminology merely would add nothing to the lucidness of men's thinking, or of teaching; but rather confusion. We should simply have another definition added to our many definitions which don't define. But should it become everywhere accepted, and by all men, that Matter is all of Nature, including Man, we should still have to speak of some Matter, or of some forms of Matter, as conscious, and of other forms as non-conscious; and thus we should really have back the old dualism which Materialism thought to have discarded. While it would still be open to the man who believes that we *may* live after death to say, that as some Matter lives, and feels, and thinks now, so would there be nothing in the adoption of a new nomenclature for old phenomena, to preclude the expectation that the *conscious* part or form of Matter might go on living and feeling and thinking when the *non*-conscious forms of Matter are dissolved into dust. For consciousness is *force*,—the only force we really know,—and force, we are told, never dies.

The intellectual heavens have been threatening to such expectations for some time. The profounder researches that have been prosecuted within half a century in the fields of comparative anatomy and physiology, especially as to brain structure and function; "the acknowledged presence and power of the imponderable forces in mental phenomena;—the pathology of the mind having become almost wholly merged in that of the body; the growing conception of Nature as ordered and ruled in all her departments by fixed or uniformly operating laws";—all these theories and conclusions have, in effect, been the allies of the Schools which deny that there is any good ground discoverable, or as yet discovered, at least, on which to rest a hope of immortality for man.

Yet are the principles and canons of spiritual philosophy as impregnable to-day as ever they were. We know a little more than our forefathers knew as to the forms and functions of material organisms, but we are no nearer than they were to the identification of Mind with Matter. We are told of the "high charge of nervous power" in certain human constitutions, of "waves of emotion from cerebral centres," of the eminently "glandular character of the tender affections"; from all which one might be tempted to conclude, that *mind* is fast being reduced to physiological function. "But, in truth, we are just as far from discovering the real Thinker and Actor in all this commotion of nerves and brain as we were before. Nay; if we could render the human body transparent, and could thus watch all that goes on within it, what we should see would not be sensation, thought, affection, but some sort of movement, merely, among the constitutional particles of our bodily structure"; which movement of molecules were no more *mind*, however, than the revolution of a wheel is the steam that propels it.[1]

[1] Much of the language, and some of the illustrations of

The talk of the Materialist about molecular groupings, or atomic activities, really explains nothing, therefore. The utmost that he can affirm is the uniform association of two classes of phenomena; not that the two classes are only one class, or that one class—the unconscious—is the cause of the phenomena of consciousness. A *condition* it *may* be, for the time now present, but not the *cause*. In the frank words of Mr. Tyndall, "the connection of soul and body is as insolvable in its present form, as it was in the pre-scientific ages."

Our fears were futile, then. The Mind, Soul, Spirit, is not "a discredited myth." The "bundle of attributes" which we designate by one or other of these words, is antithetical to the "bundle of attributes" which we designate Matter. We cannot even dispense with the old terminology, therefore, as Mr. Huxley once told us that we might. Soul and Body are terms which represent essentially different "bundles of attributes," Mr. Tyndall being witness. It were verbal recklessness to say that we may fittingly use the one term for the other.

It remains, then, that we may still avail

---

this paragraph are Mr. Martineau's, I feel quite sure. But from which of his writings I got them, I cannot now say, or discover.

ourselves of all the old lights which guided our forefathers to faith in God and Immortality, and among them "the Light of the world." For if we are allowed, without caveat, to cite Socrates in witness to truth pertaining to "the life that now is," or to the life that is to be, we cannot consistently ignore the testimony of Jesus.

V.
ON EXISTING DISSENSIONS BETWEEN SCIENCE AND RELIGION.

V.

ON EXISTING DISSENSIONS BETWEEN SCIENCE AND RELIGION.

I PREFER the word dissensions in this connection to the word *antagonism*, or to the word *conflict*, chiefly because it is a word of milder import. Prejudices may be incited by the use of epithets stronger than are required, in the discussion of questions which divide public sentiment. Quite sure am I, that mischief has been done by the loose way in which such words as conflict and antagonism have been bandied about of late, between men bent upon assaulting the Christian Faith, and the men who have set themselves to defend it.[1] There is really very little mutually opposed feeling that deserves to be called antagonism,

---

[1] The late Dr. J. W. Draper had a fondness for such verbal excesses; a large part of the argument in his book on "*The Conflict between Religion and Science*" being conducted upon the assumption, that the Christian Religion is responsible for all the follies and wrongs of Ecclesiasticisms. Mr. Tyndall, with his candor and love of accuracy, speaks, in a note to his Apology for the Belfast Address, of Dr. D.'s work as a description of the long-continued struggle between science and *the Romish Church*:—as some of my readers may have remarked.

between worthy representatives of the Science and the Religion of our own time, I am fain to hope; but frequent occasion of *dissension* is no doubt encountered by the worthiest representatives of the two classes. How serious soever such differences may seem, however, they must spring, of course, from an imperfect or a confused conception of things, or from an unskilful handling of evidence; not from any essential occasion of conflict in the Divine Cosmos, which, as ordained and ruled by one MIND,—for the writer assumes a Theistic position—must needs be at perfect agreement in its order and action; though we may never be able to discover the concord, thoroughly, here, or to construct a synthesis exhaustive of all the mystery in the " constitution and course of Nature." The most we can do in such direction, perhaps, is to gather up confirmations of an intuitive faith in the prosecution of our researches, eliminating false factors in our endeavors to make out the mighty equation, so nourishing patience till the great illumination shall come.

The interpretation of Nature is a vast and a very difficult business. No wonder, therefore, if the interpreters sometimes fail to agree in their conclusions, or that they *dis*agree very seriously at times; especially when the attempted interpretations are *ex parte*, in spirit, or in method, or in aim; as so many of them are, it may be feared, whether attempted in the interests of Science, or in the interests of Religion. The want of an intelligent, pliant catholicity in the prosecution of the great task, has been most afflictingly marked hitherto in the *religious* advocate. The average clergyman is in a confused state of mind in respect of these things; the more liberally minded of the order finding it hard, I suspect, to reconcile old professional commitments with truths of a heterodox import which Science has forced upon the acceptance of the thinking world very generally to-day.

The vocation of the Christian Teacher is daily becoming more difficult to follow, indeed, with anything like a complete mental serenity. His position is peculiar, in that nearly all the lines of the higher controversies of the time converge upon it. None of the sister professions require such a breadth and variety of culture, or such a generosity and elasticity of sympathy, for the efficient following of it, as that of the Christian Teacher. Men in other professions may confine themselves to studies which fall within more or less definite dimensions, feeling little or no concern in the settlement of questions seemingly foreign to their respective spheres. Discoveries may be made which may threaten to revolutionize an old order of things in one professional province, which in no way affect that of another. But the Theologian sits, so to speak, at the centre of radii which connect him with the vast circle of universal truth. There is scarcely a question debated in the schools in the settlement of which he is not concerned. Hence frequent occasion of disturbance for him, or for his Faith. The brotherhood of which he is a member might live in tolerable quiet, could they be allowed to mark out for themselves a little lot of territory, and to say to all other thinkers and workers—"Now, this is our plot in the great vineyard: let us cultivate it in peace." But, alas! for such intellectual husbandmen; and alas! for all who so long for tranquillity in the higher callings of men to-day. That which they covet cannot be conceded. For one class of thinkers are compelled to intrude upon ground claimed by others; they, the intruders, being obliged to suffer intrusion upon theirs.

The provinces of Science and of Religion overlap each other, at frequent points, and over considerable spaces. "Division of labor" is expedient, and helpful to human progress, in some departments of human industry; but no such division of labor is possible, in the intellectual world, as will allow the Theologian, or the man of Science, to lay down his postulates, and to elaborate his processes, and to formulate his conclusions, irrespective of caveat or criticism from his professional rival. It is vain, in other words, to say, as some of our religious apologists are saying just now,—"Let Religion and Science each follow its own course without interruption, or jealousy." Such counsel is vain, I say, since the domain of Nature, including Man, is one. The truths discovered in this or the other section of that domain may seem independent, to enthusiastic disciples in contending schools; professional vocations of all sorts having ofttimes a blinding effect upon the minds of the men who "have their being" in them; yet is there not a single truth in any field of inquiry that can be justly claimed by any school or profession as exclusively its own; knowledge of which fact ought to have a liberalizing effect both upon men of Science and upon Theologians. Let the *Theologian* take the fact to heart; for it is he, with his fellows, who asks, most imploringly, at times, to be let alone in undisturbed possession of his peculiar postulates and principles. Let Christian Apologists know, that they cannot, as Mr. Maurice once said, "go out to parley with men of Science with a white flag in their hand, saying—'If you will let us alone we will do the same by you. Keep to your own province; but do not enter ours. The reign of law which you proclaim we admit—outside of these walls: but not within them. Let there be peace between us.'"

Yet have timid Theologians been urging this sort of compromise of late, as the best resort available to Christian "believers" in the present intellectual conflict of arms. A favorite form of such pleading for peace is this:— "The Bible was not given to teach Science: those who accept the doctrines of the Holy Book, cannot, therefore, be fairly summoned to defend them in the court to which Science makes its appeals." Now, there is pertinent truth, no doubt, in this plea; truth that might be found helpful in delivering all parties to the debate from confusion of mind, and from bad temper; had all of them courage to accept the position assumed in the plea frankly, and sufficient discretion to apply the principle asserted wisely; with the requisite readiness of mind to accept all possible consequences.

"The Bible was not given to men to teach Science": that is the bold broad proposition; a proposition charged with timely, inevitable truth. Inevitable, because the writers of the Bible had no Science to teach, in the sense of the word Science as we use it to-day, at least. But had they been rich in such possessions, it was not in the line of their vocation to use them. They had something fitter and more serviceable to do, in their ministry to the generations of men among whom they lived. There are statements in the Bible, more especially in the older writings comprised in the Volume, of *a scientific bearing;* in the explanation of which the Science of to-day might claim to be heard, should its representatives ever deem it worth while; but nowhere in the Book is there any *Science,* properly so called. For Science is knowledge, sifted, certified, formulated; and the writers of our so-called "Sacred books" had no opportunity of attaining to such knowledge. The ages in which they lived had very little of such knowledge. But had the writers of our Biblical books been in possession of all the scientific knowledge of the several ages in which they lived, and had they incorporated it in their writings, it would have been of little avail; or it would have been misleading, to after generations of men; for the Science of one age has been foolishness, in large part, to later ages, through the whole educational process of our race. Only by the intrusion of causes that would have changed the whole economy of human life, could acquisitions destined to be made by men in later periods of the world's progress, have been anticipated in behalf of the writers of Hebrew or of Christian Scriptures.

Conceding the claims of those who believe in a special revelation of God's mind to men, we must yet say, that only truth they could never have discovered of themselves has ever been so made known; all other truth having been left to come forth to view through the ordinary laws of human progress. Or men have had to toil for it, finding deposits of the precious treasure at intervals only, as men find costly gems. So far is the complaint that the Bible has no reliable Science in it, or that what there is in it is inaccurate, from being of any force as making against the claims of the Book to a Divine authorship, the alleged fact ought to be construed as guaranteeing the Bible's validity; coming as the venerable Volume does come, with "the image and superscription" upon it of the widely diversified times in which the writers of its different sections lived. By men knowing and weighing these things, the conclusion will not be counted alarmingly unorthodox, I take it, to say that Moses, Jewish prophets, or Christian Apostles, were neither Astronomers, nor Geologists, nor Physiologists, nor Natural Philosophers, beyond what their respective times admitted of.[1] It is weak and unworthy, therefore, for their disciples of our own time to fall into a fresh spasm of fear on every advance in scientific discovery. Such perturbations have been frequent in the Christian world, but after generations have invariably smiled at them.

But while the proposition, "the Bible was not given to teach Science," has the germ of a truth of some consequence in it in the controversy between Theologians and Scientific Sceptics, the inference drawn from the proposition is a glaring *non-sequitur*. Believers in Divine Revelation may very fairly be called upon to tell us, I think, how inaccurate statements of a scientific bearing in the Bible can be shown to be compatible with claims preferred in behalf of the Book as infallible; the obligation being still heavier upon the religious Apologist to explain Biblical statements which the Science of our time counts among the myths of the world's childhood. There are frequent statements, or assumptions, in the Holy Book, notably in its earlier chapters, which requires such apologetic handling to

---

[1] "It does not follow that Christ was an impostor because Moses was not an astronomer."—SOAME JENYNS.

render them even intelligible to the disciplined apprehension of men to-day:—the origin and evolution of things, to wit: the presence of death on our globe, the aboriginal unity or variety of the human race, the myth or fact of the "fall," the origin and development of language, the phenomena of the "deluge." The men who accept the Biblical versions of these marvels, requiring us to accept them just as they are given in our Holy Scriptures, cannot waive the demand aside for some elucidation that might render them less incredible than they seem to our modern Mind.

In the discussion of these and such questions, both parties, the Theological and the Scientific, have equal right to be heard; neither having authority to arrest inquiry when becoming troublesome to the doctrinal partialities of the one or of the other. The Theologian must here condescend to deal with cool passionless evidence, abstaining from all abuse of counsel on the other side;—a hint in rebuke of a temper too prevalent in "Defenders of the Faith." To betray such a spirit toward any who bear themselves worthily in the intellectual strife just now prevailing, is offensive. An Apologist of clear insight, and of good culture, will welcome all thinkers, in whatever spheres they may pursue their callings, as fellow craftsmen;

in no way trying to repress the utterance of any honest conviction, nor to evade any legitimate inference, how adverse soever to traditional beliefs, or to current orthodoxies.

But neither has the Scientist, on the other hand, any right to deem the Christian Apologist an intruder on this broad ground of mixed questions. In the attempt to deduce the genesis of Man from a monad, for instance, or in the efforts of the Materialist to resolve all mental phenomena into physiological function,—in these investigations spiritual Philosophy is as directly and as fully concerned as Physical Science is; and may fairly claim to be heard, therefore, in the valuation of the evidence submitted; all lovers of truth having abundant occasion for rejoicing at the mutually jealous watchfulness so provoked. For there is constant need, in every department of thought and experiment, to guard against the *idola tribus;* one effectual check upon which sort of beguilement, is supplied by what we may call the professional hostilities, which have marked all ages of active thought; the partisans of rival schools being thus compelled to be careful in shaping hypotheses, and reserved in asserting conclusions. Some of the more ardent of these partisans, on the one side and on the other, have been provoked to unseemly anger in these strifes; but the 'breezes' awakened by the factions have winnowed a good deal of chaff from the wheat of a wholesome philosophic truth.

We cannot cut up the territory of the intellect into professional sections, then, upon any such terms as shall leave either Scientists or Religionists at liberty to hold their respective conclusions as independent, and final. The doctrine of neutrality, for which some of our Christian Scribes plead so pathetically to-day, is a poor expedient in the interests of peace. No such compromise is possible between Science and Religion; a good deal of the ground over which the great debate must needs range being common to both; the lines which mark it out into sections being conventional merely, for the more thorough cultivation of the whole area.

All investigators into observable phenomena, all who labor to coördinate discoveries, with all who seek to interpret the meanings and purposes of the known facts and functions of the manifold organism which we call Nature,—all these are co-workers with the world's Spiritual Teachers, and are to be honored with these as contributing to the end professedly desired by all. Some of these thinkers and workers have been animated by another spirit, at times; professional prejudices having distracted the judgment and embittered the temper of the prophets; dogma and denunciation having supplanted evidence and argument in the contentions of the Schools, too often. But by an increasing number of men these things are regarded as abhorrent to the calmly judicial Spirit which ought to preside over debates which aim at "the reconciliation of Science and Religion," —to repeat one of the amiable platitudes of the time.

Hitherto the advance toward a better understanding between Scientists and Religionists, has been seriously hindered by the rigid conservatism of Theology. The education, the mental atmosphere, the routine reverence, the habitual resort to dogma, the pleasing conceit that he and his brethren are favorites with the Deity,—all these things have been unfriendly to the growth of a large and liberal thought in the Theologian. He has therefore been, as a rule, a persistent foe to free inquiry, ever, and everywhere; either as sinful in itself, or as perilous to faith and piety. The fable of the ostrich has been verified in him. Preferring safety in darkness, as he has dreamed, to danger in the light, he has occupied himself in stopping every chink in his sanctum through which a solitary ray of the surrounding radiance might possibly find entrance.

No well-informed, fair-minded man will deny, however, that this stolid religious conservatism has conferred substantial benefits upon the world; especially when opinion and feeling affecting true religion have been giddy, or when heresies of a really serious sort have been in fashion. At such times, men not lightly given to change have been very serviceable, in holding on to truths that might otherwise have been carried away in the rush. Such service has no doubt been sometimes rendered by the Theologian. In an uncertain shifting world, he has been the one steadfast imperturbable witness for what he has deemed immutable truths. He has believed all along, that, though the heavens might dissolve, and the earth pass away, there are some things here that never change, and that cannot be changed—" the same yesterday, to-day, and forever"; in support of which attitude the Theologian has had reasons to allege, some of which are unanswerable. As when he has said, for instance, that had Theology yielded to every demand of a capricious Science,—for Science, in the hands of its expounders, has often been capricious—Theology's disciples had been driven to distraction; while their teachers must have been unceasingly occupied in temporizing readjustments of their doctrines and canons. While something might be said also in behalf of religious Conservatism suggested by the nature of the truths it claims to have conserved; which, as being *moral*, mainly, and as having Divine sanctions—as Orthodoxy holds—and as having been witnessed to by reliable witnesses for ages, and rendered sacred to the affection and trust of so many millions of the human race, ought not to be too readily surrendered, the Theologian has held; and reasonably so, I think. Courageously asserting the special trusteeship of such truths, Theology has set her face like a flint against storms of adverse criticism, and sometimes against more terrible storms of persecution; and, to every demand to yield any fraction of what she has held to be "the Truth," she has returned a speedy and an emphatic *non-possumus*. And those men are blind who can find in history, or in life as we know it, no occasion for such stubbornness; while they are unsympathetic souls that are empty of all admiration of such a persistent moral bravery.

But, unhappily, Theologians have not been content to abide within these tolerably impregnable lines. It has not sufficed for them to bear their testimony to immutable truths;

but they have invaded debatable territory, in a spirit which usually animates polemics; claiming the right to decide controversies with which Theology has had little to do, and which many of its advocates have been pitifully incompetent to handle in debate. This unwise forwardness in religious Apologists has been due, very largely, to their confounding the *variable* with the *constant* contents of "the Faith"; they having somehow been led to assume,—and in some of them the assumption has been a fiery conviction—that the honor and efficacy of Religion are bound up with the credit of a crowd of miscellaneous questions, ill-assorted, ill-defined, and of doubtful import to the best informed; many of these questions, with the solutions which the Scribes had given to the world, being, from their very nature, liable to revision.

In this way Religion has been involved in all sorts of needless complications; many of her representatives having so demeaned themselves as to have fastened a bad reputation upon her among liberally-minded men. Hence it is, spite of what I have said as to the obstinacy of Theologians, that the history of Theology, or of the contests she has waged with Scepticism of various phases, is so largely a history of "change of base," or of ignominious retreats from positions she has found to be untenable. Hence, too, the strangely diversified attitudes which her disciples present before our own eyes toward the active thought of the time; the more prudent among them seeking refuge from sceptical assaults in the doctrine of "open questions."

But that was the only available position from the first for "believers," according to the terms of compromise upon which I was commenting a little while ago. "The Bible was not given to teach Science," we were assured. Well: let the Theologian hold on to and insist upon that, and he may sleep in peace, so far as his trouble might be found to spring from criticisms of his "Sacred Books." He need not then be nervously anxious about the possible meanings of certain monosyllables in those documents, or about the number of acres submerged by the "Deluge," or about the cubic capacity of Noah's ark, or about the presence or absence of a cipher in "Exodus," "Chronicles," or "Kings"; his "doctrines of grace" being in no way involved in the fortunes of such questions, as he then may come to perceive. "Let comfortable people who know no sorrow," said a late magnanimous man, "trouble their brains as to whether sixty, or six hundred, thousand fighting men came with Moses out of Egypt. We care not for numbers. What we care for is, not how many came out, but who brought them out."[1]

Yes: for that sort of free handling of the Sacred Record must the Christian Apologist be prepared to-day, holding all such incidental matters as open to review; or, need being shown, to correction. For say that he believes the Record to have consisted originally of the *ipsissima verba* of its reputedly Divine Author; yet cannot the fact be disguised that it was put into the world in such shape, and subjected to such conditions, that no man of sense can insist upon every jot and tittle of the Record, as we have it now, as of infallible authority. The mutabilities of time are traceable in it; Scribes have imported "improvements" into it; while theological necessities have seemed to justify dishonest dealings with it: which facts might well dispose the stoutest believer in the integrity and authority of Divine Revelation, surely, toward a tolerance of opinions hitherto disallowed by our Orthodoxies. By any man competent to discuss these questions worthily, it ought to be admitted that it is far from a dangerous concession to say, that contentions about matters

[1] The Rev. Charles Kingsley.

such as those I just now instanced, may be decided this way or that without imperilling the faith of Christendom in the Gospel of Jesus Christ.

But the ordinary type of the Theologian would seem to be constitutionally averse to open questions. Truth for him must have no ravelled edges. The far-spreading areas which research has explored, in parts, in the past, and over which adventurous Thought claims the right to range to-day,—these areas the Church has closely fenced in; the limits being clearly defined in her Creeds and Catechisms; no discovery within the vast enclosure being allowed to pass into general acceptance without the Church's sanction. Hence the authoritative airs of the representative of the Church as he delivers himself from the pulpit, commonly. He has so long played the part of Sir Oracle that he brooks not a whisper of dissent, but deals out dogmatic decisions with most imposing assurance; closing all troublesome questions with a waive of his priestly hand; hinting at alarming consequences in another sphere for all who doubt his word! It is really afflicting to hear, indeed, how every little stammering talker in a pulpit to-day will presume to claim the sanction of the Church for his ignorance, or for his conceit. But sadder yet is it to be compelled to confess, that many of the men who occupy seats of high ecclesiastical influence among us, look coldly, or with antipathy, upon some of the best authenticated results of modern research:—a very pitiful fact, surely, for the closing decade of a marvelously progressive century, as we count this Nineteenth.

But yield we must,—for I too am of the illiberal fraternity—and much, or we shall provoke our own children to scorn. Great concessions have already been wrung from Theology. We of this generation cannot conceive how great a thing it was for religious Apologists to be constrained to allow, that Moses, as well as later Biblical writers, wrote, not actual, but phenomenal truth only, touching matters pertaining to Physical Science, as when they convey the idea of the Earth's being a *plane*, and not an oblate spheroid, as we have long known it is; but men abreast of the critical culture of our time are prepared for a considerable advance upon that. Some of them are frankly saying, indeed—Christian Scholars being among the frankest of them—that the "Sacred writers" sometimes wrote simply *traditional* truth, in dealing with matters pertaining to *historical* Science. Nor to intelligent Christian men should the concession seem alarming. The literatures of all peoples begin with myths, and are continued in legends; the Scribes of later times gathering up the legends, and weaving them into their narratives without formally distinguishing the legendary items from those which we should now call historic. The capacity so to distinguish is attained late in the intellectual development of a people; even in that of its most progressive minds.

Nor do I see how we can make the claim good, that it must needs have been essentially otherwise in the growth of critical ability in the Hebrew mind; except by assuming a continuous miraculous direction of its workings. Such an assumption would be of no avail, however, with the literary productions of the Hebrews with which we are here concerned under our eyes, and subject,—as they are, of right—to the critical implements and methods that are applied to all other literatures. The actual application of these to the books of the Old Testament has long since shown us, that in them are to be found, as in all the literary productions of the world's intellectual childhood, mythical imaginings, and romantic inventions, and poetic decorations—as all duly-equipped and candid Scholars now admit; those whose hearts would still cling to the notion of a continuous miraculous inspiration and supervision of the Biblical writers, being compelled to acquiesce in the conclusions of Historical Criticism as to these things.

Nor ought these heavy demands, as they may seem to some, upon Christian believers, to be construed as supplying just occasion for disesteem of the Bible as a whole, or of its essential contents. For when were men ever in a position to stipulate with the Creator, that any special directions He might deign to make known for their moral guidance, should be absolutely free from all traces of human ignorance or frailty, in the form in which they should be made known to, and conserved for after ages? Or upon what grounds can we justly insist to-day, that we will not practically accept the revelation of His mind and will which as Christians we claim to have in the Bible, except upon the assumption that the Book holds no material whatever of an inferior value or authority? Do not the principles postulated and expounded at large by Butler, in Chap. iii., Part II., of the "Analogy," show us very convincingly, how a Christian man may admit that there are fabulous admixtures in our Holy Scriptures, while continuing to revere these Scriptures as given and inspired for our help and salvation?[1] For it is not these incidental inferior elements in the make-up of the Divine Book that we revere, but those which make up its immutably Divine substance, with the heavenly tone and drift of the Book;—'tis these things we love and trust in the Scriptures; knowing how to account for very undivine things being there, with perfect composure of mind.

The concessions I am here pleading for must be made soon, if we would prevent increase of mischief to the cause of Religion among the reading and thinking classes of Christendom. Faith is giving way under the strain put upon it by our Rabbis, by their resisting demands which a riper culture has been making for sometime. Some of the more liberally minded among them allow it to be silently understood, I know, that not all that was once imposed by the Church upon the faith of disciples is necessary to be received now, before a man can claim the title of a Christian. But that is a cowardly way of dealing with the new issues; some of which I have been elucidating.

[1] "Neither obscurity, nor seeming inaccuracy of style, nor various readings, nor any disputes about authors of particular parts, nor any other things of the like kind, though they had been much more considerable than they are," (the great dialectician might have added unverifiable legends) "can overthrow the authority of the Scriptures."

Meanwhile the Church, as a whole, goes contentedly on, reading out to those who gather in her synagogues the cosmogony and the anthropology ascribed to Moses, and the amazing longevities of "patriarchs," and the philologically curious story of Babel, with the arrest of the sun and of the moon on their march through the heavens at the bidding of a Hebrew warrior; just as if nothing had happened since the nursery days of human development to discredit such stories, or to render them less fit for Christian edification than they were once held to be.

Still worse is it, for unskilled teachers in our Seminaries to be insisting upon the literal truth of such stories, to crowds of young people who gather about them. For these young people, or their like, on attaining to larger knowledge in the school of the world, discover that much that was taught them in their undiscerning years is unreliable; all faith being abandoned, often, in the struggle with sceptical objections which for many of them ensues on their going forth into life; their religious instructors having done nothing to fortify them for such struggle. A good deal of the infidelity, indeed, in the manhood and womanhood of our time, has a tone of angry protest in it, against the imposture—as it is often counted—practiced upon their childhood by teachers who carefully kept all difficulties beyond the ken of their youthful disciples; or glossed difficulties over with glosses which even children soon come to see through.

But more pertinent to the special purpose of this paper—and far more important—is it to add, that it is just here, in the investing of the legendary or merely poetical things read in the Bible with essential and permanent truth, that most of our trouble with the Science of the time originates. There is very slight occasion left to fear for, or to fight about, things of a really vital importance to Religion in our Holy Scriptures. Christ has come into human history never to go out of it again. His truth is in the very air we breathe, and will animate all coming generations of men. His Church, too, will ever have work to do, as an educational institution, and as a refuge for souls in the time of trouble.

But, unhappily, we Christians are encumbered with an inheritance from remotely past ages, of another sort from that bequeathed by Jesus. In addition to things of a moral and immutable value in our Divine Directory, orthodox theologies require us to accept a crowd of apocryphal things; all which, in the popular religious estimation, are massed together with things forever reliable under the title of "Inspired Truth"; inspiration being commonly taken, with a strange logical looseness, as including, or as drawing after it, *infallibility!* Whatever dissension, or antagonism, or conflict, may exist to-day between the representatives of Science and the men who speak in the name of Religion, has its chief provocation in, and is mainly fed by, this indiscriminate estimate of the "Sacred Records"; which estimate both Religionists and Scientists blindly persist in assuming to represent no more than the essential contents of our Christian Faith;—to the very sore damage of its reputation.[1]

I am chiefly, almost wholly, intent in this paper, upon commending the spirit of a large and pliant tolerance to both parties in these high debates, by showing how much may fairly be claimed by this party or by that, and how much must be granted by the one, or by the other. But my animadversions have hitherto been almost exclusively directed against the

---

[1] "The books and traditions of a sect may contain, mingled with propositions strictly theological, other propositions, purporting to rest on the same authority, which relate to physics. If new discoveries should throw discredit on the physical propositions, the theological propositions, *unless they can be separated from the physical propositions*, will share in that discredit." *Macauley*, on "Ranke's History of the Popes."

intolerance of Theologians. The severe things I have said have not been meant for all the masters in our Schools of Christian Thought, however; among whom may be found those who combine with their faith in Divine Revelation, a courageous confidence in the most adventurous scientific explorations, believing in, and themselves following eagerly in quest of, the harmony existing between the Works and the Word of God, as they divine. By these nobler representatives of religious Apologetics are exhibited, not infrequently, a liberality of thought, and a generosity of sympathy with modern progress, with an openness of mind to new truth, and candor in the examination of alleged facts, and a magnanimity of temper in the discussion of rival theories, not always found in men of Science.

Nor have the more timid of the disciples of Theology, whom I have had chiefly in view in my caveats, done all they have done in resistance to our "new learning" without provoking occasion. The world has been made acquainted in recent years with a new species of dogmatism; all the more offensive because marking the utterances of men who have so vigorously denounced dogmatism, as hateful in itself, and as a hindrance to the discovery, or to the dissemination, of truth. A priesthood of Positivism has arisen among us, as narrow and intolerant in temper as the priesthood of the old faith ever was; and which, being denied permission to suppress "superstition" by force, has given vent to its detestation in an imperious scorn. Proclaiming through the press, or from the professorial chair, the gospel of a relentless Fate, or commending to our deepest trust the working of a self-evolved and automatic mechanism, they deny the *possibility* of the existence of a Maker and Ruler anywhere in space. Cordially crediting matter with prerogatives we should once have called Divine, they deride the notion of an inspiring MIND, building their altars to a grim sort of god they call Force, or Law.

The facts which they set in array in support of their faith are ofttimes imposing enough, but, as under all new and fervid inspirations, there is a marked lack of logical coherence between their *data* and the conclusions which the *data* are made to yield.[1] Impatient of research, or when research fails them, our new masters make out their case by resort to the speculation they are wont to decry; flinging across every chasm in their schemes the bridge of a baseless hypothesis.

[1] "The logical feebleness of Science is not sufficiently borne in mind." *Professor Tyndall.*

They despise old creeds, but they revere new formulæ. Fugitive opinions are made to do service as immutable principles. Mere modes of operation, or groups of conditions, are accepted as exhaustive explanations of mysteries which they do but suggest. Or as the Duke of Argyll puts substantially the same allegation, in his "Reign of Law":—"The mere ticketing and orderly assortment of external facts, is constantly spoken of"—by our shallower scientists, he means,—"as if it"—this assorting and cataloguing of phenomena—"were in the nature of an explanation; and as if no higher truth in respect to natural phenomena were to be expected, or desired."[1]

Yet this style of thing passes for Science, with the many, to-day; and that because of the oracular tone assumed by the men who declaim these things; while men of some discernment among us are often charmed out of all regard to the truth or untruth of so-called scientific statements or conclusions, by the high-sounding rhetoric in which the high priests of Positivism so much excel. One of these, and a man of vast and varied learning too, tells us that "Life is a continuous adjust-

---

[1] "Oh Law! Law! most abused of scientific terms: what an infinity of dogmatic illegalities are committed in thy name!" *W. L. Thornton;* "OLD-FASHIONED ETHICS," p. 120.

ment of internal relations to external relations." But what do we gain from the luminous utterance, to add to what our forefathers knew when they talked of the "animal spirits," and of the "vital fluid"? Why do bodies gravitate toward each other? it is asked in catechizing learners in the schools from which superstition is excluded. Because God willed it, another Cowper's Cottager might answer. "No," says the presiding oracle; "but because they attract each other." But, to my apprehension, the answer of the master of learning sheds no more light upon the mystery he thus waives aside, than the answer of an ignorant piety.[1]

We doubtless know more than our earlier ancestors knew, of the *interdependence* of things in the great Organism with the order and workings of which Science occupies itself, or of the *relations* of many of its parts to other parts; but the forming and the informing Energy ever escapes detection. There is something back of, or beneath, that order and those workings of which Science, as distinct from Philosophy, can tell us nothing. Analysis conducts to the *unknown:* to that which is unknown to scientific scrutinies, at least; Mr. Tyndall very frankly confessing, in one of the

[1] See Janet's "*Final Causes,*" note p. 142, Edin. Ed.

many passages of a rare literary beauty and power in his writings, the incompetence of his own school to close the debate between spiritual Philosophy and Materialism, with any authoritative utterance adverse to the former. "Science is mute" here, says our modern Master of Words;—in the contention as to whether there is any Power back of or above the material mechanism of the universe, that is;—but adding a question which hints at what he would fain say, I suspect: "If, then, the materialist is confounded and Science is dumb, who else is prepared with a solution? To whom has this arm of the Lord been revealed? Let us lower our heads and acknowledge our ignorance, priest and philosopher, one and all."[1]

Well: the attitude were becoming to the highest among us, while the confession would be good for the wisest; but, unhappily for those who would leave the matter there, the irrepressibly inquisitive Something within us will not let us rest in the agnosticism thus touchingly commended to our acceptance. Men have ever and everywhere asked, as they are asking still with a resolute persistence — *Whence? Why? Whither?* Materialism would have us be content with settling the

[1] "Fragments of Science," p. 421, Appleton's Ed.

how of things about us, and in us, and abroad in space; but to the extent that Materialism should succeed in prevailing upon men to occupy themselves wholly with asking and answering the question How, Science would stagnate and decay. No: inquiry cannot be arrested because the Agnostic tells us he can go no further; any more than at the warning of the Theologian that his "Sacred ground" must be respected. The final *How* of the Materialist suggests the *Whence*, and the Whence suggests the *Why*, and the Why suggests the *Whither;* and so the disciples of Materialism snap the leash in which the leaders would hold them, and the harriers are out o'er the wide-spreading plains of Philosophy, not even bating breath at what the Materialist calls "the quagmires of metaphysics"! Yes; 'tis even so: let men of feeble intellectual limb, or of a timid prudence, lament it as they may. Physiology is the pathway to Psychology; into whose misty realm we must follow the problems which an empirical Science suggests, but which it can never answer.

And that confessedly: Science, in her more temperate moods, avowing that she knows nothing of origins, or of ultimate destinations; that she has nothing to do with anything but with *processes;* knowing nothing of any

Power from without, she tells us, in any way affecting these processes. Well: let Science be content with saying that, and we shall hear much less than we hear now of dissensions between her and Religion. But ever and anon she shows restiveness within these her own self-prescribed limits; her representatives betaking themselves to the schools of Philosophy, to dictate conclusions there; denouncing all prying into things beyond their professional ken. But Science, in the persons of her disciples, is offensively presuming in all this—in so insisting that the limits to which she has come shall be regarded as impassable barriers by thinkers of all other schools—and this spite of the obvious fact that those limits are constantly changing, and spite of the fact that many of her own conclusions are as yet confessedly inconclusive. Herein the Scientist repeats the blunder of the Theologian, in *his* demanding that the dictates of Theology shall be final for all men, and for all time. Science ought to be ashamed of herself in assuming such airs; seeing that in her more candid moments she confesses, that the explanations she has to offer *of things within her own province*, are far from satisfactory; and remembering how largely she draws upon the unknown, or the "unknowable," to eke out the account she gives us of the system of Nature; and remembering, too, the differences that exist among her prophets as to what are, or what are not, incontrovertible articles in her creed.

In deciding this last very important matter we are cautioned to "take Science at her best." But how shall we discriminate between Science at her best in Haeckel, who postulates protoplasm as the only working power he needs to produce a Universe, and Science speaking through the lips of Mr. Tyndall, who tells us that the universe, or our own familiar globe, at least, once existed in a state unendurable to protoplasm?[1] This adjudication of the eminent Englishman being received as authentic, the hypothecating of another working power is required to produce protoplasm; whether the "idea" of Hegel, or the "will" of Schopenhauer, or the "absolute" of Schelling, or the "divine wisdom" of Leibnitz, who shall say? Or how shall we reconcile the bald materialism of a Maudsley, or the spontaneous-

[1] "There was a time when the earth was a red-hot melted globe, on which no life could exist. In the course of ages its surface cooled; but, to quote the words of one of our greatest *savants,* 'when it first became fit for life there was no living thing upon it.' How then are we to conceive the origination of organized creatures?"—"*Contemp. Rev.*," vol. xxix., p. 901.

Of the doctrines of the Haeckel school Mr. Tyndall elsewhere says:—"Surely these notions represent an absurdity too great to be entertained by any sane mind."

generation assumptions of Bastian, with Mr. Darwin's doctrine of a Divine inbreathing of life into two or three rudimentary organisms;[1] Science being supposed to be "at her best" in all these gentlemen? The mechanical Evolutionst, again, asks for inconceivable millions of ages for the accomplishment of the task which the fiery atoms had before them when first they began their dance in space; and Sir William Thompson (Lord Kelvin) answers that Astronomy cannot grant the time required. The hypothesis of Laplace had no need of a God, but Newton required a God to account for gravitation. The law of "Natural Selection" explains for the Darwinian the whole long mysterious advance of life, up from some simple germ to consciousness, and conscience, and will; but Mr. Wallace, a chief among the prophets in the school of Natural Science, tells us that the process stops at Man.[2]

These things are not said in derogation of the solid claims of Science. Certainly not. They are aimed, in a half-playful vein, at the fallibilities of *scientists*, not at any weakness or inconsistency in Science;—a distinction to be borne in mind in the conduct of discussions such as that I am now occupied with. A good

[1] "Origin of Species," Amer. Ed., p. 429.
[2] "Natural Selection," Chap. x., *passim*.

deal of poetry slips into the treatment of these themes, although poetry is supposed to have no place in scientific discourse; *non-*"Scientific uses of the imagination" being quite common with our Positivists. But toward *Science*, which is sifted, certified knowledge, as I have defined it,—toward this, we can entertain no disparaging feeling, of course. Of Science, indeed, we may say with Hooker in his glowing eulogy of Law:—"Her seat is the bosom of God, her voice the harmony of the world: all things in heaven and in earth do her homage; the very least as feeling her care, and the greatest as not exempted from her power."

Yet may we be permitted to repeat Professor Virchow's declaration, that there is a good deal of "unverified Science" abroad to-day; which, not being *certified* knowledge, is therefore *not* Science. While we may also take upon us to resent the pity that is so freely indulged in to-day, toward those of us who still remain in "the bondage of superstition"; that sort of thing being out of place in any intercourse taking place between scientific sceptics and men still retaining religious convictions. But to how much of such effrontery have we been treated in these later years! No wonder if believers in the old Gospel, ill-informed, as a rule, as to the causes and tendencies of the intellectual commotion prevailing about them, —no wonder if many of these men have been startled by the extravagances talked of late in the name of Science; or that some of them have been driven to assume extreme positions toward modern Thought. Yet is the fear foolish that any great interest in Morals or in Religion is likely to suffer shipwreck, or to be in the slightest degree imperilled, in the intellectual tempest said to be "raging" in our time. There has been a violent swing of the speculative pendulum within the space of fifty years from spiritualism toward materialism, from metaphysics to physics. But a reaction is already noticeably upon us; for the eternal questions are with us still, and the insatiate longings are in us still; and the former can never be answered, nor will the latter ever be laid, by a Science which resolves the secret of the Universe into protoplasm!

With nothing like scorn, or jealousy, however, may Theology regard the enthusiasm for material Science everywhere predominant to-day; for it will leave rich deposits of humanizing and elevating and refining acquisitions to the ever-increasing store of the world. Fresh discoveries, or new interpretations of old facts, will continue to seem ill-fitting to long-accepted conclusions;—whence debate and strife between intellectual conservatism and intellectual radicalism, in the future as in the past. But after generations will adjust the new to the old, as generations have ever been doing, and as we are doing to-day, with no felt discord in the whole so made up. The well-attested truths of Biology, of Chemistry, of Physiology, of Psychic phenomena, so puzzling to many of us now, will take their places in the evolving line of order as quietly, or as unquietly, as the discoveries of Copernicus did, with no sensible shock to the foundation on which Christian Faith reposes.

"Let knowledge grow from more to more," then, revealing the manifold wealth and variety of Nature, and applying its discoveries to the relief and help of Man. We acknowledge the service with all thankfulness. Only, let not Science, in conceit of her powers, or rendered vain by her triumphs, tell us that there is nothing to know or to revere in the vast Economy of which we are part except matter and phenomena! "Great God! I'd rather be a Pagan, suckled in a creed outworn," with sentiment, and reverence, and vague high hopes in me; with communings with the UNSEEN—if only of "a silent sort"—and with dreamings of a life unlived, and with struggle to attain the unattainable, than have my faith and my ambition confined within the dimensions of the materialist's curt creed. Men of a native acuteness, and of spiritual susceptibility, conscious of wants beyond the power of temporal resources to satisfy, will go on refusing to worship mechanism, or atomic activities, or electrical currents, though called by divine names. The prophetic human soul will persist in suspecting that there is a spirit in the mechanism, that the atoms are animated, that the currents are from a higher source: will persist in disbelieving that courage and cowardice, laughter and tears, the blessedness of peace, the misery of remorse, sin, guilt, shame, or truth, nobleness, sweet affections, are nothing but the blind play of molecular elements, or the outworking of a latent heat!

When the pride and the dissipation of this latest Renaissance shall have passed away, there will come, we may safely anticipate, I think, the modesty and the reverence of a more enlightened and more firmly consolidated Christian Faith. Many men are just now giddy about, while some men rave over, the achievements and predictions of contemporary Thought. There is ground for gratitude, but none for vanity, or for fear. Devout souls start up alarmed every now and then that the foundation of their hopes is going to fail, but when the vapor of the hour is past, the eternal Rock is there still.

Rock? Nay; no rock at all: nothing more reliable than fugitive sand, surely, seeing the blanched look that spreads over the faces of religious believers, on some bolder sceptical speculation being launched upon the intellectual air. "O the pity of it." For speculation is but *guessing* at solutions of mysteries; sometimes hitting the mark, but ofttimes missing it. But when hitting it "in the eye," never disturbing the confidence of sensible men in the eternal verities. Let us be patient, and forbearing, trying to possess our souls in peace when things look threatening for Christian hope. So it has been, often; yet Christian hope survives. So is it now, to the apprehensions of some of us. But "this also is vanity." Of all the questions which agitate the thinking world to-day, few will send a ripple to the farther shore of Time. Men launch their theories upon the great sea, fondly dreaming they will live through every tempest that may come; but, as with the mimic craft of children, the waters suck them in, and not even a waif floats to tell where they perished!

I have contributed nothing in this Essay toward the solution of any one outstanding problem in controversy between Religionists and

Scientists. I had no such purpose before me in sitting down to write. I am not competent to such tasks. I have been simply pleading that a broader and more pliant tolerance, with a more patient forbearance, may be habitually shown by both parties. The last word has not been spoken yet by either of them. "We do not know enough of the matter," to use one of Butler's favorite phrases.

In closing my present line of reflections and animadversions, it affords me pleasure to cite the saying of a man worth hearing in these high debates; who condenses into a paragraph nearly all that I have said in the prosecution of my chief purpose in this paper :—"He who contemplates the universe from the religious point of view, must learn to see that this which we call Science is one constituent of the great whole; and as such ought to be regarded with a sentiment like that which the remainder excites. While he who contemplates the universe from the scientific point of view, must learn to see that this which we call Religion is similarly a constituent of the great whole; and being such, must be treated as a subject of science with no more prejudice than any other reality. It behoves each party to strive to understand each other, with the conviction that the other has something worthy to be understood; and with the conviction that, when mutually recognized, this something will be the basis of a complete reconciliation."—Herbert Spencer's "*First Principles,*" *p. 21.*

VI.

AN HISTORIC FOOTHOLD FOR FAITH.

VI.

AN HISTORIC FOOTHOLD FOR FAITH.

CHRISTIANITY is an historical religion. We can place our finger, so to speak, upon the epoch of its birth in our accepted Chronology. The countries in which it had its earliest home, or which first felt its regenerating power, are there, definite and certified, in the Geography of our globe. The men whom Christianity called into public life, or with whom it had dealings, are real, tangible men, whose names and doings have place in authentic Biography. While the institutions which it founded, and the customs that it originated, are with us in undiminshed vigor to-day.

Now, to establish the truth of these claims were to render good service to the cause of Christian Faith, surely. Nor were the task very difficult; for the Christian records are of recent origin, comparatively. The New Testament is a modern book, compared with the literature of ancient India, or of Egypt, or even of Greece, in her better days. It was written, or its component parts were written, within what we call the historical limit, in the light of an advanced civilization; while the writers tell us, in the main, what they themselves had seen, or heard, or otherwise had good assurance of, and that in a plain, unvarnished way. The substance of what they tell us touching the origin and early development of Christianity may be stated within a brief compass.

In the reign of Tiberius Cæsar there appeared in Palestine a wonderful personage, who claimed to have been sent to speak with men about love, and righteousness, and eternal life; and sundry other things which the world needed to hear about. He called God His Father; told men that they were brethren; and set them the example of a beautiful and many-sided goodness. He gathered disciples about Him; taught publicly; wrought wonders; —or so the New Testament narrative represents—but, provoking the anger of the rulers of His people, He was put to a cruel death; the Roman representative of the time assenting to the taking off. The record goes on to tell us, however, that on the third day after that He rose again from death, and ascended to heaven; and that His disciples, inspired with a strange enthusiasm, perpetuated the system that had seemed crushed by the crucifixion of its founder. Spite of bitter persecutions, the movement, thus reanimated, rapidly enlarged itself; men of all grades and of all tribes accepting its doctrines, social and political influence coming more and more under its sway; till, at length, the civilized world came, almost wholly, to be called after the name of the Man who had been put to death on a little hill just outside of Jerusalem!

Such is a brief and rapid-running outline of the story which we have in the New Testament, of Jesus, and of the beginning of the religion that bears His name. For Christian believers in general it is sufficient; the story having marks of truth in it most convincing, to all who will examine them fairly and in a right temper; while the witness of the Christian Church to the same effect is unanswerable. Yet has the question occurred to us, no doubt, on hearing or reading of these wonders:—What has the history of the outlying world of the time to say to these things? Are there any testimonies to their truth to be found outside the literature which Christianity created? Did the proclamation of the Gospel wake any echoes in places and among peoples beyond the limits of Palestine? Has Christ any other witnesses than Evangelists and Apostles? Or did He come and go unnoticed except by His disciples and friends? Now, to minds of a certain temperament, these are questions of immense interest. From sympathy with such men—men of an inquiring, sceptical disposition, some of whom may possibly take this book in hand—I am going to answer these questions in the affirmative, as best I can within the narrow space to which I must confine myself. To Christian believers, some of them not well informed as to these matters, possibly, it may prove a gratifying discovery, should I succeed in making the claim quite evident, that the great facts of their religion are found, not only in authorities which, being interested, might be suspected of partiality, or of a too easy credulity; but in authorities free from all possibility of suspicion of such sort attaching to them: in Jewish and in Pagan writers, for instance; who, if they give us any testimony in any way favorable to Christianity, must have given it unwillingly, or unwittingly. But can any such testimony be produced? The following pages will supply an answer to that inquiry, in part, at least.

The materials available for such service are but scanty, it must be confessed. The wear and tear of well-nigh twenty centuries have wrought immense ruin among the literary treasures of antiquity. Once abundant, they are now few and fragmentary; which fact will explain, very largely, why we have so little in secular history bearing upon the presence and operations of early Christianity in the world. The scantiness of such testimony was once, and for a time very clamorously, alleged as an objection to the credibility of the New Testament records. The objection is scarcely ever heard to-day, however; Historical Criticism having done so much in recent years to establish the reliability of those records. Yet was it not wholly unreasonable to have supposed, that the commotion which Christianity is represented as having created in the very heart of the world's civilization by its earlier life and work, would have left very marked traces in the writings of those times. The truth is, however, that to-day we find comparatively few such traces. But all that remains to us of ancient literatures is but little, as I have just intimated.

In addition to this consideration it should be borne in mind, that there was very little in the ministry of Jesus or in that of His Apostles, to attract the attention of the great world without. Palestine's place among the nations was too obscure; its people, the Jews, of too little importance. No writer in Rome, or in Alexandria, or in Athens, in the first century of our era, would arrest his pen to make note of the last rumor that had come thither as to the doings of people in Judæa, or in Galilee; people who had for long been esteemed insanely superstitious by Pagan nations.

To which facts we may add another in explanation of the matter. Let it be recollected, that the secular writings that have come down to us from those early days, are from men who were strangers or adversaries, to the Gospel of Jesus Christ; and there will be less occasion for wonder left why the writers tell us so little about the Christian movement of their time. Religious aversion would blind the eyes of a Philo to its importance; while Pagan writers would look upon it as merely a new phase of an old fanaticism, and would dismiss it accordingly.

We have parallels, I may remind the reader, moreover, to the supposed difficulty with which I am dealing. Socrates was in some respects the most conspicuous figure in Athens for a considerable period; yet Thucydides, the very prince of historians, has not a word about him. Plutarch is very far from being a merely mythical personage; and yet, though the contemporary of Juvenal, Seneca, Quintillian, Suetonius, and the two Plinys, he is never once mentioned, or in any way referred to, by any one of them; while Plutarch himself, though a voluminous writer, nowhere makes the remotest allusion to any one of them, or to their productions![1] But the references that we have in ancient authors to Jesus, or to His work, though comparatively slight, will be found of interest, I trust,—or those that may be selected—in elucidation of the theme I am handling.

And first we may cite the Jewish historian Josephus to our aid. He was born about the year 37 of our era—about four or five years, that is, after the date assigned to the Ascension of Christ—and lived till he was twenty-six years old in Jerusalem. He must have been familiar, therefore, with the contentions and struggles of the infant Christian Church with the Jewish rulers of the time. He had probably heard the whole story, substantially, of the life and death of Jesus; with incidents in the lives of His leading associates. That is manifest from what he gives us of such memorials. He sketches the career of John the Baptist: says that he was a preacher of virtue; that he baptized his proselytes; that he was imprisoned, and put to death, by Herod Antipas. He tells us, also, of "James, the brother of Him that

[1] Mr. Emerson, in Introduction to the "*Morals*," Ed. Little and Brown.

was called Jesus," and of his being put to death. But the supremely valuable bit of information to Christian believers which Josephus affords, is the testimony that he gives us to Jesus Himself. And we may now be permitted to cite the celebrated passage in evidence, since the latest and greatest of Semitic scholars, M. Renan, concedes, in his Life of Jesus, that the testimony is substantially genuine.[1] "At that time," says Josephus, "lived Jesus, a wise man, if He may be called a man; for He performed many wonderful works. He was the teacher of such men as received the truth with pleasure. He drew over to Him many Jews and Gentiles. This was the Christ.[2] And when Pilate, at the instigation of the chief men among us, had condemned Him to the cross, they who before had conceived an affection for Him did not cease to adhere to Him; for on the third day He appeared to them alive again. And the sect of the Christians, so called, subsists to this time."[3]

[1] "*La Vie de Jésus*," Introduction, pp. 40, 41,—a book which fired the public mind with an enthusiasm for questions which some years before were deemed superannuated. But, upon the whole, the book is a Romance, rather than a Biography.

[2] M. Renan suspects that the passage ought to read—was *called*, ἐλέγετο, Christ.

[3] Jos. "Antiq.," xviii. 3.

Such is the testimony of the great Jewish historian, to facts which lie at the foundation of Christian Faith. Not the testimony of a *friend*, but of an *enemy*, of the Gospel; who must have inwardly detested what must have appeared to him as a pestilent heresy, no doubt. He could have told us very much more to the same effect, we may safely infer, I think; for these are merely side-glances, so to speak, from the prosecution of his chief purpose; which was to write the history of his own people and nation, from an orthodox standpoint of the then prevalent Israelitish belief. Yet how significant are the statements and the allusions in the passages I have just cited!

Names and events familiar to Christian ears are found in these Hebrew *Memorabilia* also; in their proper places, and in their proper order: names which link themselves to other names which Josephus does not give us; events which require other events to explain them;— for which explanation we must go to the New Testament, however. John the Baptist had survived, in his reputation, at least; his work, and the death he died are on record elsewhere than in the Gospel histories. There is a "James" also commemorated, who was a "pillar" in the infant Christian Church, as we learn later from St. Paul. But the testimony of Josephus is fullest and most explicit to the "Head" of the Church:—to the miracles He wrought, to the style or the spirit of His teaching, and to the cardinal fact of His resurrection. While he tells us, too, of the persistent devotion of His disciples, and of the perpetuation of the "sect" of those who were called Christians. Why, we have here, the reader will note, nearly all the ground facts of the Gospel; and the witness to the whole was a contemporary of the first Christian apostles, whom it is impossible to suspect of partiality for Jesus, or for His doctrine; all which testimony we may now receive as reliable, or with only slight qualification.[1]

I have got from the Jew all that I intended to elicit. He has many more items which I might turn to purpose; but enough. Let a man of yet greater eminence in the world of letters now take the witness stand. Let a Pagan take the place of the Jew.

Tacitus, the Pagan I proceed to call, was born about the year 60 of our era. He must have known, of course, of the new religious

---

[1] "To demand, before admitting the authenticity of a writing, not only direct quotations in a contemporary book, but also multiplied attestations that these quotations are neither invented nor mutilated, is to accept as history nothing but legal documents and official patents." E. De Pressensé: "*Jesus Christ: His Times, Life, and Work,*" p. 111, Amer. Translation.

movement in the East, which by his time had spread itself widely over considerable parts of the Roman Empire; for frequent rumors and reports of its doings and progress in those parts, would reach Rome by way of Brundusium, or Ostia. Nay: but he knew of it, as we shall soon see, through its increasing prevalence in the metropolis itself. Yet he makes no formal allusion to this Christian movement. It was merely as incidental to the order of his narrative of other affairs, that Tacitus condescends to notice at all what he probably esteemed another outburst of Hebrew fanaticism. His testimony, like that of Josephus, is the more valuable, therefore; from its having been given incidentally, simply. And this is how he came to give it.

Twenty-seven years after the crucifixion of Christ, Nero burned Rome—in reckless sport, it is said by some. But certainly not personally, or directly, for the Emperor was elsewhere when the ruin was wrought. But the odium of the deed somehow attached itself to Nero. To divert, therefore, an inflamed public attention from himself, he provided a crowd of "fictitious criminals," to use Gibbon's phrase. He caused to be seized and to be put to torture "an immense multitude of men," says Tacitus. Who were these men? The author of the "Annals" will tell us. They were men, says he, "whom the common people called Christians." The reader will mark, *en passant*, the amazing fact that comes out here; that within some thirty years after the death of Christ His followers were *multitudinous* in Rome! But who or what were these Christians, to the apprehension of the historian? He will tell us. "*The author of the name,*" says he "*was Christ; who in the reign of Tiberius Cæsar suffered death by the sentence of the Procurator, Pontius Pilate.*" Why! we are here reciting the very words of the Apostles' Creed; though written by the pen of a heathen historian, who was thus unconsciously vindicating a cause which he despised. Despised, I say: for note, my reader, how he proceeds. "This pernicious superstition, (*exitiabilis superstitio*) thus checked for the time," —checked by the crucifixion of Jesus, as was hoped—" broke out again, and spread, not only over Judæa, where the evil originated, but through the city also,"—Rome. . . . "Accordingly, the first who were apprehended confessed; and then, on their information, a vast multitude were convicted. And when they were put to death, mockery was added to their sufferings; for they were either disguised in the skins of wild beasts, and worried to death by dogs, or they were crucified, or they were clothed in some inflammable covering, and when the day closed, they were burned as lights to illumine the night."[1]

A fearfully tragic story, but confirmed by very pathetic testimonies which the Roman Catacombs have preserved from ancient days down to our own. As we tread the gloomy labyrinths which stretch for miles beneath the city on the Tiber, to which Christians betook themselves in times of persecution in the earlier Christian centuries, and where they buried their dead,—there we may read to-day by the light of the torch in the hand of our attendant, the confessions of faithful souls in multitudes to the truth and the preciousness of Christ's religion; which rendered victims of Nero's, or of Diocletian's wrath, or of the wrath of some other imperial tyrant, triumphant over death in its cruelest forms: credentials, these, beyond all possibility of suspicion. Much of the testimony of antiquity to primitive Christianity has been devoured by the hungry teeth of Time, as I have said; but in the catacombs, death and the grave are eloquent in attestation of its presence and power in the then metropolis of the world! And

---

[1] Tacitus: *Annals xv. 44.* "The most sceptical criticism is obliged to respect the truth of this extraordinary fact, and the integrity of this celebrated passage of Tacitus."—GIBBON.

men who thus suffered and died for their faith, had not been followers of "cunningly devised fables."

Another Roman historian, of unquestionable credit, gives us two or three items of evidence of an affinity with that of Tacitus, touching the credibility of early Christian records.

Suetonius lived and wrote in the latter part of the first century of our era, and the first third of the second century. His work on the "*Lives of the First Twelve Cæsars*" survives, with a fragment on Grammarians and Rhetoricians. In his life of Claudius, who reigned from the year 41 to the year 54, he tells us that he, the Emperor, banished all Jews from Rome; which statement precisely corresponds with one which we find in our book of the "Acts of the Apostles."[1] This measure was meant, as we learn from our author, to relieve the city of the disturbances that were continually arising among the Israelites within its bounds; the instigator of these tumults, or the chief occasion of them, being one Chrestus, as Suetonius relates.[2] He penned this brief incidental remark in a light, passing way, we must assume; having had little intimate

---

[1] Chap. xviii. 2. "Claudius had commanded all Jews to depart from Rome."

[2] *Judæos, impulsore Chresto, assidue tumultuantes, Româ expulit.*

acquaintance, of course, with the people he was writing about, or with their interior affairs. For to him the Jews resident in Rome at the period would be about what the Jews of the Ghetto were to the better classes of the great city down to a comparatively recent time; or still more obscure and despised. Not unnaturally, therefore, Suetonius betrays some confusion, or lack of discrimination here, springing from his necessary ignorance. For among these Jews he is telling of, would be many *Christianized* Jews in the later years of Claudius. But these the author of the "Lives of the Cæsars" would not be able to distinguish from the majority of their countrymen, in dealing with the records or traditions that had come down to him. All would be numbered and spoken of as Jews. Now, between these two classes, the orthodox descendants of Abraham, and the followers of the Galilean, frequent debates and strifes would ensue, such as that we read of as having taken place at Corinth some years before;[1] the orthodox Hebrews defaming and persecuting the renegades from the customs of Moses; sometimes putting here one and there one to death, we may safely assume. It was these contentions and *émeutes*, no doubt, with more serious disorders

[1] **Acts of the Apostles, Chap. xviii. 12–16.**

springing out of them, at times, which moved the Emperor to drive out of the city all these troublers of its peace.

Now, during these contentions the name of Christ would often be heard, of course. That name was really the occasion of all the strife; the Christianized Jews maintaining that *Jesus* was the Christ, the orthodox Jews vehemently denying it. Thus it came to pass, that, by outsiders, who knew no more as to what these foreigners were wrangling about than Gallio did on the occasion of the tumult at Corinth, and cared as little, this Christ, Christus, Chrestus, came to be thought of and spoken of as the *impulsor*, the chief instigator, the ringleader, of all the disorder. For I identify, and that on good authority, Suetonius' Chrestus with our Christ; the two names differing very slightly; they having frequently been confounded, or the one having been used for the other, by ancient heathen writers.[1]

We thus get from Suetonius an express testimony to important facts and incidents in early Christian history. While he gives us more in his Life of Nero, (*cap.* 16) where we read—"*The Christians were punished*" by

---

[1] Tertullian takes the heathen writers and speakers of his time to task, in his *Apology*, C. *3*, for their so carelessly writing or pronouncing Christus Chrestus.

that cruel prince. Aye; punished, indeed, as Tacitus has just told us in lurid lines. But our present author seems to hold that they, these Christians, were punished because they were "men of a new and magical superstition," as he designates them. Yes; *new*, certainly, is this so-called superstition. Only two very short reigns, of some seventeen years taken together, since that of the man under whom the Founder of the superstition was put to death; but thus early the capital of the world is agitated by the presence of His disciples.

But why *magical* superstition? A word flung out at something but dimly or confusedly discerned, probably; vaguely hinting, it may have been, at the *religious rites* of the Christians, so strange and offensive to Pagan peoples hearing of them; their meetings for worship being held in the night, or very early in the morning, and in secret places; when unnatural and abhorrent things were done, rumor said. Or traditions may have survived, and got abroad, of marvels, miracles, having been wrought by the Founder of the new sect:—the sick healed by a touch, demons cast out, the dead restored to life: and how could these things have been but by the arts of the magician, to the apprehension of a Pagan? Or the word *maleficæ* used by Suetonius here, may have had for him in his using it, its general etymological signification of *evil-doing*, simply. For had not this reputation fastened itself upon Christians almost everywhere at that time? Hating the world, they were hated by it:—"*odium generis humani*," as Tacitus pronounces; all sorts of misdemeanors and crimes being attributed to them, when scapegoats were wanted for imperial or popular passions to wreak themselves on. The Founder of the *superstitio* was a malefactor, or was so reported of. How easy to conclude, therefore, that the *superstitio* itself was *malefica!* In one or other of these ways, we may construe Suetonius' denunciation of the sect of the Nazarenes.

But for the loss of historic documents, we might have had to-day in our hands testimony still more explicit than that of Tacitus to the truth of New Testament statements. For we read in one of the early Christian Apologists, of a State Paper, then preserved in the archives of Rome, it would appear, entitled the "*Acts of Pilate*"; such Paper purporting to be a report made by the celebrated Procurator to his Imperial master of his administration of affairs in Judæa; in which the miracles and the crucifixion of Jesus were spoken of. To such a document Justin Martyr appeals, at least, in his Apology presented to the Emperor, Antoninus Pius, and the Roman Senate, about the year 140; where he says,—"And that he did those things, you can learn from the Acts of Pontius Pilate."[1]

This document—the "Acts of Pilate"—has perished, however, assuming that it once existed; but we have a Paper of like import in the letter which the Younger Pliny addressed, while governor of Pontus and Bythinia, to the Emperor Trajan; in which letter he asks counsel as to how he should deal with those men of his province who were charged with neglecting the Pagan temples. "I have never had to deal with this kind before," says the imperial Deputy, "and I know not what is the custom to pursue: whether any distinction is to be made in respect of age, or whether those of tender years are to be treated the same as adults: whether pardon is to be granted on repentance, or whether it is useless to cease to be a Christian: whether it is the *name* that is to be pursued, even when exempt from crime, or that the crime is to be attached to the name." What a singular question! Crime

---

[1] The writings of Justin Martyr:—"*Ante Nicene Christian Library*," Clark's Ed., p. 47.

Tertullian, in his Apology, about the year 200, confirms the reference of Justin, saying—"Of all these things, relating to Christ, Pilate, in his conscience a Christian, sent an account to Tiberius, then Emperor."

attached to a name otherwise wholly free of reproach! How vividly one is reminded of words spoken some years before Pliny's time: —"Ye shall be hated of all men *for my name's sake!*"

The guilt of these Christians, Pliny goes on to say, "they confessed to be this: that they were accustomed to meet on a stated day before light, and to sing a hymn alternately to Christ, as a god; and to bind themselves by an oath, not to the commission of any wickedness, but not to be guilty of theft, or robbery, or adultery, never to falsify their word, nor to deny a pledge committed to them, when called upon to return it." "When these things were performed," said these Christians under examination, "it was their custom to separate, and to come together again to a meal, which they ate in common, without any disorder." Indeed! Well might Pliny be puzzled in having to do with offenders of such sort. He knew of men taking oaths: oaths of conspiracy against the government he represented, and in other desperate plottings; but here were men taking oath *not to commit any wickedness!*

Yet had the governor of Bythinia only a confused notion, probably, of what he was just here writing about. From more intimate knowledge of Christian usages than he could then have had, however, we can shed light on some of his vague allusions. The "meal" to which he refers was the "Lord's Supper" (or the Agapæ, possibly); the observance of which Jesus had enjoined, as we know, upon His followers for all time. While we know well, also, what was meant by the "oath" he mentions, or how the report of oath-taking had come to his ears. Among Latin-speaking peoples, the word by which the Holy Supper was early designated was *sacramentum;* which also meant, which *commonly* meant, indeed, in those times, an *oath*. What Pliny refers to, therefore, we may safely decide, was what we still call *the sacrament;* in the receiving of which those primitive Christians vowed allegiance to Christ, as Christians do to-day the world round. And so great was the number of those who did this, that Pliny complains that the heathenish temples were all but empty! What a marvellous revolution in such a brief space of time! Who was its author? By what power had it been accomplished? These early disciples of Jesus have told us through the pen of a Pagan philosopher. "They were accustomed to sing a hymn *to Christ, as God.*"

Support is lent to Pliny's representation of the condition of things in his province during his administration, by a writer who flourished a little later; who states, in a book bearing the title of "*Alexandrus*," that in his time Pontus was "full of Christians." This author, Lucian, was born about the year 125, at Samosata on the upper Euphrates. A scoffing philosopher, a severe satirist, but an acutely clever man, he traveled far and wide in quest of knowledge touching everything then knowable; becoming a bright, witty, fertile scholar. In his wanderings and sojournings in various cities he came upon Christians, of course; otherwise learning much about them. Yet has he nothing but scorn for them; using the knowledge he gathered about them as material for insulting caricature. Some of his statements or allusions are very notable, however, in their bearing upon the subject I am treating in this Essay. In his work "*De Morte Peregrini*," a satire upon voluntary martyrdoms, then so common, he makes fuller and more explicit reference to the disciples of Jesus than elsewhere. His hero, Peregrinus, Lucian represents as playing the part of a hypocrite at Antioch; joining the Christian society there, rising to the dignity of a bishop through the skilful, agile way in which he demeaned himself, but holding his religious associates in contempt the while; speaking of them—in Lucian's fiction, the reader will bear in mind—as "miserable men; who, hoping for immortality in soul and body, had a foolish contempt of death, and suffered themselves to be persuaded that they were brethren; because, having abandoned the worship of the Greek gods, they worshipped the crucified Sophist, living according to his laws." Pope Alexander VII., in 1664, placed Lucian's "Peregrinus" in the index of prohibited books; "yet even beneath the satire," as the Rev. A. S. Farrar remarks, "we rather hail Lucian as an unconscious witness to several beautiful features in the character of the Christians of his time: viz, their worship of 'the crucified Sophist,' their guilelessness, their brotherly love, their strict discipline, their common meals, their union, their benevolence, their joy in death. His satire is contempt, not anger, nor dread. It is the humor of a thorough sceptic; which discharged itself on all religions alike, indicating one type of opposition to Christianity: viz, the contempt of those who thought it folly."[1]

Much more might be gathered from non-Christian sources in support of the position I am trying to make good, as the basis for a

---

[1] "*Critical History of Free Thought,*" being the "Bampton Lecture" for the year 1862. Lect. II.

conclusion of some consequence, as I hold, to Christian Faith. What I have already done, however, may suffice to that end. The citations are trite to scholars: I simply aim to bring them into more general recognition; chiefly in correction of a type of infidelity which continues to assert, or to insinuate, that Jesus is a Myth, that Christianity was palmed upon the credulity of ignorant ages by priests, or that the Christian Christ is only the Krishna of Hindoo mythology, transferred to another age and another clime! With such notions there is not much likelihood of Scholars being seriously infected to-day; but in infidel circles *not* scholarly, such notions are still current. Historical Science has done something for us, how much soever it may have unsettled.

Yet could the men whose testimonies I have been reviewing have known little more of Christ than His bare existence; with certain facts and incidents, rumors or reports of which would naturally get abroad. For very much more we cannot reasonably look to Roman historians, or to Greek satirists, or to men whose minds were charged with aversion toward, and with hatred of, the new Sect. These men, at best, saw Christ only at a distance, so to speak; or heard of Him only through uncertain or perverting media. For a fuller and more faithful portraiture of Jesus we shall have to go elsewhere: to men who associated with Him closely, and saw Him familiarly, and heard Him through sympathetic ears:—"*men who received the truth with pleasure,*" to recur to Josephus' characterization. We shall have, in brief, to bring the Christian Scriptures in evidence.

And why not? It may be to refute them, or to find them put to confusion in the hearing; but we cannot consistently wholly ignore them. Of course not. In historical investigations, since Niebuhr wrote, we miss no item of significance seemingly the smallest; we lose the track of no hint, though leading into mist and quagmire; while we listen with acute ear to testimony the most remotely bearing upon the end we are trying to reach; never willingly or knowingly suffering the slightest deposit of prejudice to abide in the mind, while prosecuting any line of inquiry we have in hand. Simple fairness would therefore require that we hear the Evangelists and Apostles of Jesus in this debate. But this I waive, if only as being beyond the scope of my original intention; merely glancing at some of the more strikingly identifying features of the delineation which we have in the Gospels.

This I may do without protest being heard, since even our "destructive" critics treat the character of Jesus as historical; but taking of it only what pleases them, or serves their purpose, and rejecting the rest. The day of Voltaire as a critic, with that of Thomas Paine, is gone. Even to Strauss, Jesus is the wise Galileean Rabbi: the being without whose presence in the mind perfect piety is impossible. To M. Renan he is "the loveliest incarnation of God, whose beauty is eternal, and whose reign shall have no end." While Goethe speaks of Him as "the divine man, the holy one; the pattern, example, and model of humanity": the life of the Saviour appearing to Mr. Carlyle as "a perfect ideal poem": the greatest of all heroes to him being "One whom he will not name, leaving sacred silence to meditate that sacred matter"; Jean Jaques Rousseau, as representing a somewhat earlier period of Free-thinking, having left the judgment on record, in his *Pensées et Maximes*, (p. 39,) that "the Gospel has marks of truth in it so striking and so perfectly inimitable, that the inventor of it would have been more wonderful than the hero."

We may look back on Jesus then as upon a real, intellectually tangible personage; and may study His character, as we study the characters of other men whom history commemorates; carefully eschewing everything in our estimate, of course, which Criticism would forbid our availing ourselves of.

Qualities were prominent in that character upon which the world has cast disdain: condescension, tenderness, pity; but to these Jesus gave conspicuous place in His teachings and life. Taking hold of lowly and despised things, He showed how much of an overlooked heavenliness there was in them. His doctrine came forth in speech simple almost as that of childhood. Passing by the sages of history, He took a little child, and set him in the midst of His disciples and on-lookers, telling the great and the wise to be imitators of him. "Learn of Me," said He, "for I am meek and lowly in heart." "Blessed are the poor in spirit," the "peacemakers," the "merciful," and even "they that mourn." How novel such doctrines must have seemed, the reader may be ready to exclaim, to an age hard, and selfish, and sensuous as that of Herod, or Tiberius! From the first, Jesus allied His cause with weakness, and with despised classes of people; a fact very strange in the founder of a new Kingdom. Going down to the level where the lowliest stood He made the ignorant and the outcast His brethren; entering into their modes of thought, making their joys and their sorrows His own, defending them against the tyranny of priests, and rabbis, and civil rulers.

There was another side to Christ's character, however, as portrayed in the Gospel histories, than that of a gentle, patient passivity. There was a vehemence and a severity in His temper, at times, seemingly incompatible with the milder attributes so prominent in Him; as when He denounced the hollowness of those who could "tithe mint and anise and cummin," while forgetting "the weightier matters of the law,—judgment, mercy, faith": or as when He pronounced repeated woes upon "Pharisees and Scribes, hypocrites"; who "devoured widows' houses, and for a pretense made long prayers"; using the language of a startling fidelity when He rebuked the appointed teachers of the nation as "blind guides," "whited sepulchres," a "brood of vipers," fit only for "the damnation of hell!"

Side by side with His humility, too, there is what we might almost call a very pronounced *egotism* in Jesus; speaking "as one having authority"; telling men to hear *Him*, to obey and follow *Him;* setting aside divine institutions as having done their work since He had come; overruling and contradicting the teachings of lawgivers and prophets; assigning no higher authority for all He did than a "verily, verily, *I* say unto you"; and all without a trace of fanaticism in the saying and doing of these things. He dared, also, did this Christ of the Gospels, to institute a Society with universal aims; sending out ambassadors to make known His will to the world, even when unable, to all outward seeming, to defend Himself against the malice that was seeking His life.

How free He was, again, of all traditional bias, of all sectarian partiality, of all national prejudice; calling Himself, therefore, not the son of Abraham, nor the son of David, but the Son of Man. Rising out of all moral limitations of time and place, of race and of religion, He embraced the world in the scope of His desire and aims. Even so. Of all prophets or teachers, of any age or country, Jesus of Nazareth was the first to break through all narrowing inherited restraints, to ignore all hampering ethnic affinities, and to teach, even in the face of an envenomed bigotry, the universal Fatherhood of God and the brotherhood of men![1]

A veritably unique sort of personage must

---

[1] The inspiration of these brief notices of Christ's character is from the Rev. Dr. Bushnell. See his "*Nature and the Supernatural*," (Chap. x.). From a comparison of Dr. B.'s treatment of the subject and my hasty sketch, some verbal identities may possibly be detected.

we hold this Son of Man to be, then, saying nothing of claims more transcendent, of which we may not take account here. Yet how unworthily has the image which the fourfold Biography gives us been treated; with what blind rage has it been insulted, at times! At one period, and for awhile, Jesus was an "impostor"! but this chiefly among men embittered by the wickednesses of Ecclesiasticism. The men who started, or who circulated the foul allegation soon grew ashamed of it, however. It is therefore discarded now, except by a vulgar unbelief. It does not answer the purpose of its inventors; it will not fit into all the wards of Christ's character; it originates for the unbeliever more difficulties than it solves for Him. Here was an impostor with no discoverable motive for His imposture: an impostor who despised worldly gain and glory, who preached the blessedness of self-denial, who said that purity and love and righteousness are the most precious things in life, who bribed His followers by promises of poverty and persecution, and who laid down His own life in attestation of these precepts. Impostors being rarely found of this order, we hear no more to-day of the old vile imputation.

But He is next, or with others, a demented enthusiast. Not a *deceiver*, but Himself *de-*

ceived:—carried away by a frenzy born of religious broodings. Strange, this: very strange. As if the Lord's Prayer, or the Sermon on the Mount, could have come from the lips of a distempered fanatic! No: enthusiasm there doubtless was in Jesus, but with no trace of an insane extravagance about it. It was quiet, reverent, humane, discriminating; free of all those melancholy eccentricities by which we know the religious zealot in history or in life. Josephus, Tacitus, Suetonius, Lucian, with later adverse reporters or maligners of Jesus, or of His followers, did not know of these things, or they might have reported otherwise of Him, and of them. But nay: the doctrine of Jesus was too high, too heavenly, for men living in their times, with their moral vision confused and blurred by prejudice and passion, to take it in. After more than eighteen centuries of increasing fitness for the doing of that, as we complacently count, even the *Christian* world still fails to take it in.

All direct, positive testimony to the truth of the Gospel's advent into the world, and its work in it, I have left beyond regard, the reader will note, in this discussion:—the literature which the new religious life created, the institutions it built up, the victories it won over hoary superstitions, and false philosophies, and political tyrannies. Of these, with multitudes of other facts, and "conspiring probabilities," of like import, I have said nothing. I have not suffered Christianity to say a word through its mouthpiece, the Church. I have tried to be true to the aim which I expressed in almost the opening sentences of this writing:—to ascertain if the outlying, non-Christian world knew anything of the wondrous things that the Evangelists and Apostles of Jesus tell us of, at or about the time the things were said and done. That it did know something of them has been made tolerably plain, I may now presume to say. It did not know much,—how could it?—But it knew sufficient to lend credibility to the Gospel story. Enough. We have found a Christ—*the* Christ, in history, aliens and enemies being witness. And with that fact Unbelief will have to reckon.

www.ingramcontent.com/pod-product-compliance
Lightning Source LLC
Chambersburg PA
CBHW031821230426
43669CB00009B/1211